DISABILITY, THE FAMILY AND SOCIETY
Listening to mothers

Disability, Human Rights and Society
Series Editor: Professor Len Barton, University of Sheffield

The *Disability, Human Rights and Society* series reflects a commitment to a particular view of 'disability' and a desire to make this view accessible to a wider audience. The series approach defines 'disability' as a form of oppression and identifies the ways in which disabled people are marginalized, restricted and experience discrimination. The fundamental issue is not one of an individual's inabilities or limitations, but rather a hostile and unadaptive society.

Authors in this series are united in the belief that the question of disability must be set within an equal opportunities framework. The series gives priority to the examination and critique of those factors that are unacceptable, offensive and in need of change. It also recognizes that any attempt to redirect resources in order to provide opportunities for discriminated people cannot pretend to be apolitical. Finally, it raises the urgent task of establishing links with other marginalized groups in an attempt to engage in a common struggle. The issue of disability needs to be given equal significance to those of race, gender and age in equal opportunities policies. This series provides support for such a task.

Anyone interested in contributing to the series is invited to approach the Series Editor at the Department of Educational Studies, University of Sheffield.

Current and forthcoming titles

DISABILITY, THE FAMILY AND SOCIETY
Listening to mothers

Janet Read

Open University Press
Buckingham · Philadelphia

Open University Press
Celtic Court
22 Ballmoor
Buckingham
MK18 1XW

e-mail: enquiries@openup.co.uk
world wide web: http://www.openup.co.uk

and
325 Chestnut Street
Philadelphia, PA 19106, USA

First Published 2000

A catalogue record of this book is available from the British Library

ISBN   0 335 20310 8 (pb)   0 335 20311 6 (hb)

Library of Congress Cataloging-in-Publication Data
Read, Janet. 1947–
     Disability, the family, and society: listening to mothers / Janet Read.
        p.   cm. – (Disability, human rights, and society)
     Includes bibliographical references and index.
     ISBN 0-335-20311-6. – ISBN 0-335-20310-8 (pbk.)
        1. Parents of handicapped children – Great Britain.   2. Mothers – Great
Britain.   3. Handicapped children – Great Britain – Social conditions.
4. Handicapped children – Services for – Great Britain.   5. Handicapped
children – Great Britain – Family relationships.   6. Social advocacy – Great
Britain.   I. Title.   II. Series.
HQ759.913.R38   2000
306.874'3'0941–dc21   99-31549
                                                                                  CIP

Typeset by Type Study, Scarborough
Printed in Great Britain by Biddles Ltd, Guildford and King's Lynn

To Luke and Chiade

Contents

Series editor's preface

The Disability, Human Rights and Society Series reflects a commitment to a social model of disability and a desire to make this view accessible to a wide audience. 'Disability' is viewed as a form of oppression and the fundamental issue is not one of an individual's inabilities or limitations, but rather, a hostile and unadaptive society.

Priority is given to identifying and challenging those barriers to change, including the urgent task of establishing links with other marginalized groups and thus seeking to make connections between class, gender, race, age and disability factors.

The series aims to further establish disability as a serious topic of study, one in which the latest research findings and ideas can be seriously engaged with.

The struggle for rights, equity and social justice on the part of disabled children and their allies is a very difficult and relentless one. This book provides some informative and insightful accounts of the complex and demanding difficulties that these mothers had to engage with. We are given vivid insights into their qualities, abilities, satisfactions and disappointments arising from their common task of being at the sharp end of the struggle for change in a world of discrimination and disabling barriers.

There were two particularly important insights that I derived from the book. Firstly, the way Read provides a framework in which her conception of the mothers as *mediators* helps to understand and explain their position and function. They acted as buffers between various professional gatekeepers, institutions, disabling barriers and their children. This active involvement provided the mothers with a series of significant learning encounters and an increasing ability to act in an informed and skilful way. Secondly, the overwhelming emphasis of these accounts is that of the centrality of their children and the quality and degree of what the mothers have *learned* from their relationships with them. Their children changed the mothers' view of their world and of themselves. This provided a further motivation for the mothers to challenge all forms of disabling barriers in the lives of their children.

I found this book an absorbing and at times moving read. We are presented with some wonderful first-order accounts by the parents, which are rich in detail and capture the subtlety and complexity of their lived experience. The mothers' voices provide a wealth of issues to be debated, reflected upon and explored more seriously.

This book is essential reading for all those concerned with issues of equity, participation and the struggles for inclusivity. It will appeal to a wide readership and I have no doubt provide a significant number of issues to be discussed, critically explored, as well as further topics for a research agenda.

Professor Len Barton
Sheffield

Acknowledgements

I should like to acknowledge the huge contribution made by the 12 women who took part in the West Midlands study. They were generous with their time, ideas and hospitality. I also wish to express my sadness at the deaths of Jean, Rob and Margaret and to offer my sympathy to their families.

My thanks go to Len Barton for constructive comments on the draft of the book, to John Harris, Clare Blackburn, Luke O'Shea and Chiade O'Shea for reading and commenting on earlier drafts of chapters, to Angela Bolton for helpful suggestions about some of the literature, and to Cath Cole and Janis Firminger of Hereward College for supporting the project and putting me in contact with the majority of the West Midlands mothers.

Introduction

For more than 20 years, my work has brought me into contact with considerable numbers of mothers who have disabled sons and daughters. This work has taken a variety of forms. Whatever the focus of the specific task in hand, however, it has almost invariably entailed discussion of the women's fine-grained reflections on their approaches to this particular experience of motherhood and mothering. Becoming mothers of disabled children required them to give thought to and become accomplished in a wide range of tasks of which most had previously had little or no understanding and experience. It would be difficult to imagine remaining unimpressed by the ethical deliberations, the knowledge and the skill that so many brought to bear on activities which frequently went unremarked and unsung.

One strong and recurring theme in almost any discussion was the way in which mothers saw themselves as having actively to adopt the role of mediator, a buffer state between their children and other people and institutions. Time and time again they told stories of how they initiated and managed with others a difficult and sometimes painful renegotiation of their children's position. This might be with family or friends, in public places or in relation to formal institutions.

At the same time, they described the explaining work that they undertook with their disabled children: the ways that they tried to give their sons and daughters mediated accounts and reinterpretations of circumstances and events that did not always serve them well. With both modest and far reaching aims in mind, many women almost routinely made attempts to offer their sons and daughters alternative perspectives which they saw as being more protective of their interests and more in keeping with their intrinsic worth. This explaining work could often prove to be taxing and upsetting.

There is one example that for me, epitomizes many elements of what is entailed in this explaining work with children (Read 1991). A mother described to a workshop of other mothers how her young disabled daughter had asked her out of the blue, whether she had been disappointed when she gave birth to her. The child had gone on to ask her directly whether she would not rather have had a 'normal' baby. Most other mothers in the workshop or those who have heard that story since, have found some aspects of it immediately recognizable and have their own comparable stories to tell. The growing child is gradually learning the value accorded to disabled children and adults within our society. Over time, everyday experiences suggest to her that she may be regarded as less than her non-disabled peers. Without preamble, she turns to the nearest intimate adult for an explanation and for reassurance. Her mother has to set aside the fact that she finds the question unbearably painful, think very quickly and respond in a way that neither denies the evidence of her daughter's experience nor reinforces any erosion of her sense of self-worth that may be taking place.

It seemed self-evident that if mothers took on this mediating and negotiating role, it was because they saw something as being wrong, something needing to be explained, changed or rectified in some way. They felt that things could not be left as they were. There was a challenge to be made and a new balance to be struck. Their accounts of *what* they thought was wrong often had a significance beyond the immediate circumstances of their own and their children's lives. They provided an illuminating perspective on the experience of disabled children and adults more generally and on the place that they occupied in the world.

It was partly as a result of such discussions in the early 1980s that I became convinced that some of the most debilitating features in the lives of disabled children and adults were not a necessary or inevitable consequence of having impairments. In the first instance, it was the parents with whom I worked who showed me that some of the really devastating and restricting experiences which they and their children faced were socially and politically constructed and could be changed by social and political means, were there the will to do so. They sifted such ideas both in isolation and in groups at a time when few practitioners were sympathetic to them and before debates on the 'social model of disability' and social exclusion and inclusion were more commonplace (Family Focus 1984; Read 1985, 1987). Such perspectives are central to the approach I take in this book.

This project is an attempt to explore some of the distinctive features of the experience of mothering and motherhood for women who have disabled children. As part of this, I shall give particular attention to the question of their role as mediators: why this becomes an almost inevitable and necessary part of their own and their children's lives and what this tells us about the position that they and their sons and daughters are in. The book places considerable emphasis on mothers' own accounts of their experiences and their explanations of issues which shape their perspectives and guide their actions. This is not to suggest that there are no other significant versions of events and no other significant people in the households, families and communities where disabled children grow up. Listening to mothers does not carry with it any assumption that disabled children, their fathers and their brothers and sisters need no voice or that mothers can speak in their stead.

For other key players, this may sometimes be a little difficult to swallow as discussions on motherhood and mothering inevitably involve reference to other members of their households. In informal discussions that I have had about the book with both mothers and fathers of disabled children, I have detected some initial concern that fathers and fatherhood are being left out and whether this indicates a lack of respect for or underestimation of their contribution. Some parents too, have asked whether it would not have been a good thing to obtain the views of the young people.

In acknowledging the central and singular role played by mothers in the lives of disabled children and young people and in placing their accounts centre stage, there is no intention here to diminish any of the significant contributions made by others, including the children. Neither do I wish to render others passive nor reinforce stereotypical representations of their lives. While it is legitimate to enable mothers to explain why they do the things that they do, I recognize, like others, that research is needed which consults with *all* family members about their experience, needs and circumstances (Beresford *et al.* 1996).

Central to the book is a small-scale study of the experiences of 12 women from the West Midlands of England. They were all mothers who had disabled sons and daughters over the age of 16 years. Their accounts provide a springboard and a starting point for the whole piece of work. To appreciate the experience of the mothers, however, it is helpful to have an understanding of the policy context as it affects disabled children and those close to them and some of the changes that have occurred over the past two decades. The mothers refer to services and policy developments that are familiar territory to them but may not be so to every reader. For example, we can have a greater appreciation of the struggles described by one of the women, Victoria, to gain a mainstream school place for her son in the early 1980s, when we realize that major moves towards the acceptance of inclusive education are much more recent than this.

By way of introduction, therefore, Chapter 1 will cover a brief overview of that policy context and of the changes that have taken place, concentrating mainly on the past 20 years, about the lifetimes of the sons and daughters in the study. I shall also refer to those aspects of policy and practice that were established at an earlier time but which had a lasting impact on service provision for disabled children and those close to them.

It is also helpful to consider a summary of trends in literature and research over the past 20 years as part of that context or at least as closely related to it. The focus of research and the images of disabled children and their families that are projected from it, have much to tell us about the context in which the 12 women and others like them were living. Once established, theoretical assumptions and emphases in research and literature can be found to have an enduring impact even when they have been strongly challenged or refuted. There may be something of a time lag before ideas generated by research and writing filter through to practitioners and services provision. For this reason, some approaches in slightly earlier literature will be included in the overview that forms part of Chapter 1.

In order to begin the process of understanding the issues which may shape the perceptions and activities of mothers of disabled children, Chapter 2 draws directly on the accounts of the 12 mothers who took part in the study in the West Midlands. In Chapter 3, it is my intention to explore the roles played by mothers of disabled children more generally by reviewing what research on disabled children and their households has to tell us about their lives. In Chapter 4 I shall aim to augment our understanding of the experience of mothers of disabled children by considering theoretical work on mothering and motherhood more generally. Chapter 5 considers the literature on disability and oppression in an attempt to make sense of the mothers' perceptions of their children's place in the world and experiences that they routinely face. In Chapter 6 I shall suggest that when we take together the research findings and theoretical literature in the previous chapters, we gain a clearer insight into why mothers of disabled children take on the role of mediators and what is involved when they do.

 1

A neglected minority: an overview of policy and research

The UK policy context

Until the 1970s, disabled children and their families were a largely invisible group as far as politicians, policy makers and the general public were concerned. No one knew how many existed and little reliable information was held about their circumstances (Glendinning 1983; Beresford 1995). In the immediate post-war period, some children lived at home, but there were also large numbers (10,000 at the beginning of the 1950s) who spent their childhoods in the depriving conditions of long-stay hospitals (Oswin 1998). In these years following the Second World War, the problems faced by disabled children and those close to them were construed almost exclusively as private and personal misfortunes rather than issues for which there should be any great measure of public interest or collective responsibility.

It was only in the 1970s, as a result of the groundswell of public concern about thalidomide that disabled children and their families found themselves anywhere near the public policy agenda. Concern in the media and among politicians and the general public over thalidomide was further reinforced by awareness of the consequences of vaccine damage. This resulted in greater recognition of the problems of all disabled children and their families and generated some political will to take action (Baldwin and Carlisle 1994).

In addition, public enquiries which revealed appalling conditions in some long-stay hospitals for people with learning disabilities (for example, DHSS 1969) gave added impetus to policy initiatives designed to transfer the short and long-term provision for this group of service users from a hospital to a local authority base (DHSS 1971). This general trend had implications for those disabled children who had hitherto been placed in long-stay hospitals and other institutions and whose care and upbringing were also giving rise to growing concern (Oswin 1971, 1978; DHSS 1976). In the early 1970s, in addition to those in local authority and voluntary sector institutions, there were an estimated 6,500 children living in mental handicap hospitals (Oswin 1998). Tyne (1982) argues that one of the significant achievements of the National Development Group for the Mentally Handicapped, set up by the secretary of state at the DHSS in 1975, was to convince successive administrations that the large hospital could never be regarded as a satisfactory home for a child. It therefore became an even more commonplace and established expectation that children with severe physical impairments and learning disabilities should be brought up at home in their families of origin.

In 1970 under the provisions of the Chronically Sick and Disabled Person's Act, the then newly formed local authority social services departments were made responsible for a wide range of services for disabled people. The 1970 Act has often been regarded as an early example of ground-breaking legislation in relation to service provision for disabled children and adults. It is also widely acknowledged, however, that like many other innovations of the period, it fell foul of the repercussions on western economies of the oil crisis of the early 1970s. Nevertheless, this legislation was to remain an important part of the foundation of community care provision for the next three decades (Clements 1996).

In the same year, too, the Education (Handicapped Children) Act gave local education authorities the responsibility for educating those children with severe learning disabilities who had until that point, been the last group of children excluded from the right to education. The Warnock Committee, set up to investigate the education of all disabled children, also reported in 1978 (DES 1978). It introduced the concept of special educational needs and proposed a legal and procedural framework whereby provision should follow need. The resulting Education Act (1981), introduced the process which quickly became known as 'statementing' through which an assessment and statement of a child's special needs were intended to determine what was the appropriate provision – an example of the 'needs-led' approach which was to become more familiar in the 1990s. When the 1981 Act came into force in 1983, no additional funding was made available to aid its implementation and it also became rapidly apparent that the statementing process was to prove complex, protracted and costly for all concerned. Statementing remained largely unreformed, however, until the introduction of additional legislation and a new code of practice in 1994, intended to streamline and set time-limits on the procedures. Despite the hopes held out for it by some, the Education Act (1981) did not pave the way unequivocally for the inclusion of disabled children in mainstream schools.

The 1970s also saw the Court Report on child health (DHSS 1976), which highlighted the difficulties faced by disabled children and their families and made recommendations for measures to promote more integrated child health services.

In the same decade, some attention was also paid at an official level to the difficult financial circumstances of households with disabled children. As a consequence, measures were introduced, such as a number of cash benefits, to offset some of the extra costs associated with disablement and in 1973, the setting up of the Family Fund to give grants to families of disabled children.

From the late 1970s, the acknowledgement of the contribution made by parents of disabled children and the growing official respect accorded to them were increasingly reflected in policy documents and professional literature. Exhortations to professionals to work with 'parents as partners' became commonplace (DES 1978; Mittler and McConachie 1983). It was argued by some, however, that for notions of partnership to go beyond rhetoric, fundamental changes would need to take place in working practices and relations. Often it was questionable whether any such shifts in thinking and practice were happening (Potts 1983; Read 1985).

Taken together, these initiatives in the 1970s and the beginning of the 1980s undoubtedly represented an increased awareness about the 'unexpected minority' as Gliedman and Roth (1980) dubbed their American counterparts. There can be no assumption, however, that this resulted in policy and practice responses commensurate with their needs. After all, even a small input of resources or limited policy change in relation to a grossly neglected group, can be presented as a considerable move forward. As will become evident later from research, the increasing numbers of parents bringing up disabled sons and daughters at home found themselves receiving far from sufficient community-based support. Glendinning (1983) argues that significant recommendations of key bodies such as the National Development Group or the Warnock Committee were ignored, overtaken by public expenditure restrictions or implemented in a limited form unlikely to make more than minor inroads into the problems that existed.

The 1980s and 1990s saw unprecedented and wide-ranging changes in the organization and delivery of health, education and social care services across the public, voluntary and private sectors (McCarthy 1989; Holliday 1992; Cochrane 1993; Billis and Harris 1996). The post-war consensus on the nature of the Welfare State broke down and successive Conservative administrations introduced reforms designed to bring an end to what was seen as the monopoly of state provision. They sought to establish and foster competition through the creation of an internal market of welfare within and between the state, private and voluntary sectors. The Labour government, returned in 1997, began an additional and demanding programme of Welfare State reforms. Since the late 1980s, therefore, both users and providers of services have been living with a rapidly and constantly reforming service environment. These and other factors affecting the organization and delivery of services, have implications for disabled children and their families. Official reports have consistently expressed concern about problems associated with service delivery to this vulnerable group (e.g. Audit Commission 1994). In addition to the reform of services and restrictions in resources, and expanded demands and duties imposed by new legislation and policy initiatives, there is also, for example, recognition of the effect on children and their parents of the increased specialization among professionals, particularly in medicine. As a consequence, children with complex needs may receive attention from an even broader range of practitioners than ever. Because these professionals frequently operate within changing organizational and legal frameworks of baffling complexity, substantial service delivery problems exist for both service providers and users (Audit Commission 1994; Hall 1997).

Gradually across the 1980s and 1990s, there also emerged a greater focus on policy and practice designed to create opportunities for the inclusion of children with diverse needs and characteristics in a range of mainstream services and facilities (Booth *et al.* 1992; Reisser and Mason 1992; Social Services Inspectorate 1994). There has been an increasing official emphasis on support services which enable children and their families to have opportunities comparable to those of their non-disabled peers. The Children Act 1989 reflected and promoted the notion that disabled children should be included as 'children first' within legislation designed to safeguard the interests of all children. Disabled children were among those defined as children 'in need' under section 17 of the Act. New duties were placed on local authorities to safeguard and promote their welfare and to enable their upbringing by their families. Once again, the principle of partnership was emphasized. In theory at least, local authorities could provide any from a host of individual and family support services which would enhance the disabled child's welfare and opportunities. Unfortunately, the combination of resource restrictions and an emphasis on other priorities such as child protection procedures, has curtailed the development of such family support services for all children deemed to be 'in need' (Department of Health 1995).

In addition to these policy shifts, there has been a growing awareness in the 1990s of changing needs and circumstances of some disabled children and those close to them, as well as the impact of significant social trends. For example, in recent years greater numbers of low-birthweight babies and those with severe and complex disorders are surviving and are being cared for at home. Many such children are 'technologically dependent' and as a consequence have very significant support needs. This has implications both for their families and for services trying to meet their needs (Lawton 1989; Baldwin and Carlisle 1994; Beresford 1995; Hall 1997; McConachie 1997). Concern has also grown about ways in which the increased general trends in childhood poverty, unemployment, the restructuring of the labour market and the greater incidence of lone parenthood may impact particularly harshly on households with disabled children, adding to their pre-existing economic disadvantage (Blackburn 1991; Williams 1992; Baldwin and Carlisle 1994; McConachie 1997).

It is evident that during the past two decades significant legislative and policy changes have taken place in relation to disabled children and those close to them. As will be equally apparent from the review of empirical research later in this book, however, it would be extremely unwise to assume that the positive impact of such policy developments has been felt universally by the children and their families. It is clear that services remain patchy and underfunded and as a consequence, children and their families are often predominantly reliant on their own personal coping resources and strategies for much of what they need.

Literature and research: an overview

There is now a substantial body of literature which offers us insights into the lives of disabled children and those close to them. The bulk of this has been generated since the early 1970s. The research field has not, of course, remained static. Fresh theoretical perspectives come to the fore and these serve to reinterpret previous work, highlight its limitations and promote new directions. The literature also reflects emerging social trends, changing characteristics and circumstances of the population of children and their households as well as reform of the law, policy and practice.

In the period up to the early 1970s, a limited amount of systematic and detailed investigation had been undertaken into the needs and circumstances of this hidden and neglected population (for example, Hewett 1970; Young-husband *et al.* 1970). Some of this work not only highlighted the extreme pressures and social isolation experienced by the children and families concerned but also raised questions about the nature of the services that they were offered and the attitudes of those providing them. In this, as in many other fields at the time, studies that placed the views of non-professionals, including service consumers, centre stage were rather unusual. Offering people the opportunity to speak as experts on their own lives had not yet gained favour. Researchers who adopted such an approach earlier than most often found themselves out on a limb, as Newson (1981: 170) explains:

> It was in 1958 that we initiated our longitudinal study of child rearing attitudes and practices in 700 Nottingham families, later to be extended to families with specific handicaps, and from the beginning we were sustained by Allport's then unfashionable suggestion that if one wanted to know what people were thinking, feeling and doing, one might do worse than just ask them.

This is not to suggest that there was a vacuum in research and writing on disabled children and their households in the 25 years following the war. The mainly professional literature which emerged during this period has, however, been the subject of considerable criticism. It has frequently been suggested that much of it misunderstood fundamental issues about the lives of disabled children and their families and that those damaging misconceptions were in turn, passed on to professionals whose job it was to support them (Roith 1974; Darling 1979; Wilkin 1979; Philp and Duckworth 1982; Thomas 1982; Glendinning 1983; Read 1985; Baldwin and Carlisle 1994).

Attention has been drawn to the ways in which a very great deal of this earlier material concentrated on personal and psychological variables to the exclusion or neglect of almost all other issues. A psychoanalytic orientation frequently provided the theoretical underpinnings. Consequently, parents' and children's experiences were likely to be explained within the limited parameters of intrafamily or intrapsychic functioning. As Philp and Duckworth (1982: 39) point out, the effect was to 'narrow the range of definition of family effects so as to implicate essentially personality and psychological processes within the family unit'. Further, the manner of construing mothers' and fathers' beliefs and reactions often lacked an appreciation of the ways in which people's individual feelings and behaviours are, in part at least, products of wider social, political and cultural circumstances and discourses (Philp and Duckworth 1982; Read 1985).

However, it was not merely that this approach was seen to be narrow in its focus. It has also been argued that there was often a marked tendency to be judgemental towards parents and to pathologize them without sound justification. For example, Cantwell *et al.* (1978: 273–4), reviewing the literature on the significance of family factors in relation to childhood autism, raise questions about characteristics frequently attributed to the children's parents:

> Numerous pejorative epithets have been applied to the parents of autistic children. They have been described as cold, undemonstrative, formal, introverted and obsessive ... The parents have also been considered overprotective, symbiotic, indecisive, lacking dominance and showing 'perplexity' or psychic 'paralysis'.

It was not only frequently suggested or implied that a disabled child produced a dysfunctional family, it was also argued powerfully that in some instances, the reverse was the case. In the 1950s and 1960s, for example, the mother of the autistic child could easily find herself held responsible for her son's or daughter's condition (Badinter 1981).

In the 1970s and 1980s, a growing number of writers began to question how substantial was the evidence of the oft-alleged deviance on the part of mothers and fathers of disabled children; concern also began to be expressed about the confusion in this earlier literature about what might be regarded as pathological and normal (Hewett 1976; Darling 1979; Philp and Duckworth 1982; Glendinning 1983; Thomas 1982; Read 1985). Darling (1979) comments on the ways in which contemporary British and American literature problematized parents of disabled children. She points out that not only was the literature replete with examples of parents who, it was asserted, were quite unable to cope, but writers also appeared suspicious of those who appeared to be handling the situation and often utilized notions such as 'over-normalization' or 'well-disguised rejection' to explain away their apparent ability to manage. In other words, they could not win. Critics also began to challenge the usefulness of well-established concepts such as 'guilt' and 'acceptance' ubiquitous in post-war writing and practice (Roith 1974; Thomas 1982). Parents were assumed to feel guilty for having a disabled child and the guilt was further alleged to be a force that drove their actions and lifestyles in ways too innumerable to count. Similarly, professionals often saw the notion of acceptance or non-acceptance of the disabled child as a rather pervasive, central and ongoing matter for the parents and the practitioner.

The choice of these ideas as central issues for practice is likely to have had more to do with the theoretical orientation of the practitioners at the time and less to do with the expressed needs and experiences of the clients concerned. Thomas (1982) characterizes much of this earlier post-war literature and

practice as hemming in parents of disabled children with universally applicable forms of victim-blaming while belittling their attempts to make sense of
their experience. Problems were defined in such a way as to require certain
sorts of professional help to aid their resolution. He further suggests that in
their search for the pathological, writers routinely ignored the conventional
features of family members' lives. This, he argues, had little to do with the
families' lived experience and everything to do with both professionals' vested
interests and their assumptions about the impossibility of disability ever co-
existing with things ordinary.

While it cannot be assumed that the typologies embedded in the earlier professional literature were extinguished, the 1970s and 1980s also saw a change
in the direction of research in this field. The Family Fund research team was
set up in the wake of concern over thalidomide; they and other academics with
a similar orientation (for example, Bradshaw *et al.* 1977; Butler *et al.* 1977;
Bradshaw 1980; Stacey 1980; Glendinning 1983; Baldwin 1985) began to put
an influential and lasting stamp on the approach to researching households
with disabled children. As Baldwin and Carlisle (1994) report, the Family Fund
also provided for the first time a mass of information about the needs and circumstances of families and the paucity of support available to them.

The researchers, often from the social sciences rather than the professions,
shifted the focus from those concerns which had previously dominated the
literature. They explicitly rejected existing professional paradigms which
assumed that severe disablement in children invariably went hand-in-hand
with individual and family pathology, and concerned themselves with other
matters:

> The assumption here is that severe disablement almost invariably creates
> practical problems. Providing help with these can relieve stress on
> families and enable them to function, as far as possible, like other
> families . . . We outline the basis for help as of right rather than as an
> expression of community concern.
>
> (Baldwin and Glendinning 1981: 124)

Without neglecting the pressure that the parents of disabled children were
under, they also stressed the individuality of those children and the diversity
of rewards, stresses, happiness and disappointments that they, much like
many other children, brought with them (Baldwin and Glendinning 1981).

This new and influential school of researchers saw parents' perspectives as
an essential dimension and they set about asking parents not only about their
own and their children's needs and experiences but also about the usefulness
of existing services. Moreover, and perhaps most significantly, they attributed
as much authority to the parents' opinions as to those of others. It is this body
of mainly empirically-based literature, started in the 1970s and 1980s and
further developed in the 1990s, on which we have come to rely to provide
information about the lives of disabled children and those close to them. The
insights that it yields into the lives of mothers of disabled children will be
explored in detail in Chapter 3.

Across the 1980s, the disabled people's movement gathered strength in the United Kingdom and a literature on the new politics of disablement was becoming established. The 1990s have seen a rapid expansion of research and publications by disabled academics and other writers within and allied to that movement. This literature has had a profound effect on the whole field of research and writing on disability.

A central concern of this literature has been to find appropriate ways of theorizing disability. Major paradigm shifts have been advocated. Increasingly, there has been a challenge to what is seen as the overmedicalization of people, experiences and events and there have been calls for theoretical frameworks which acknowledge that some of the most restricting and damaging features in the lives of disabled children, adults and those close to them are socially constructed. The theorizing of disability has increasingly been located within debates on social oppression and exclusion, civil rights and citizenship. (Morris 1991; Baldwin and Carlisle 1994; Barnes and Mercer 1996; Oliver 1996). This general literature on the politics of disablement has been one of the major influences affecting recent research and writing on the experience of childhood disability and will be considered in more detail in Chapter 5.

In recent years, along with an acknowledgement that services for disabled children have been constrained by too narrow a medical and educational focus (McConachie 1997), there has also been growing resistance to research and professional literature which represents disabled children as tragedies or burdens (Read 1991; Goodey 1992; Beresford 1994). There has been an increased commitment, enshrined in the Children Act 1989, to consult all children about matters that affect them and more awareness about the limited degree to which the opinions and perspectives of disabled children themselves have been sought (Baldwin and Carlisle 1994; Social Services Inspectorate 1994). Some researchers have become alert to the ways in which disabled children have been cast in an unduly passive role (Priestly 1998). As a result of this, there has been a growth in work which attempts to obtain disabled children's accounts and opinions directly and considers appropriate ways of involving them as active participants in research and development (Kennedy 1992; Marchant and Page 1992; Minkes *et al.* 1994; Lewis 1995; Beresford 1997; Ward 1997). A great deal of work in the 1990s also reflects the greater focus on policy and practice which create opportunities for the inclusion of children with diverse needs and characteristics in a range of mainstream services and facilities (Booth *et al.* 1992; Reisser and Mason 1992; Social Services Inspectorate 1994).

Finally, in recent years there has been greater emphasis in research on the ways in which disability, gender, ethnic origin, age, sexuality and social class should be seen as major mediating factors which differentially structure the experience of individuals and groups (Twigg and Atkin 1994; Butt and Mirza 1996). It has also been made increasingly explicit that membership of a marginalized group may have considerable detrimental consequences for individuals concerned in that it adversely affects their chances of gaining access to services that meet their needs (Baxter *et al.* 1990; Begum 1992; Langan and Day 1992; Thompson 1993; Dalrymple and Burke 1995; Shah 1997). The Children Act 1989, for example, placed a requirement on local authorities to give due consideration to children's religious persuasion, ethnic origin and cultural and linguistic background, in the way that they fulfilled their powers and duties.

Research and theory clearly has a considerable part to play in this book but at this point I want to sound a cautionary note about its impact in some respects. The reason for reviewing theoretical work both in this and later chapters, is that it can aid our understanding of mothers of disabled children and their situations as well as the ways that they are characterized by others. It can cast a fresh light on the ordinary, the familiar and the taken-for-granted. Even when we reject theoretical ideas that we regard as partial, misguided or unfinished, there is often reason to be grateful for them. As Brecht had it in his 'Song About the Good People', when someone lays a stone in the wrong place, we by watching them, see the right place. Being theoretically adventurous often entails going out on a limb to look at something in a new way, a process that almost inevitably results in misplaced stones.

However interesting and illuminating some of these developments may be, it seems important, nevertheless, not to overestimate the impact of *certain* theoretical debates on those outside the immediate environment in which they take place. For those who are intimately involved in developing a particular theoretical discourse either because of a passionate set of beliefs or because it is their job to do so, it can feel all-encompassing and far-reaching. There is nothing intrinsically wrong with this of course, unless they mistakenly believe that *this* context, *their* world, is *the* world. Many theoretical debates take place within a very confined space and rarely see the light of day elsewhere. In addition, there is frequently a gap between the abstract language of theory and the everyday language which the subjects of research and theory use to analyse their own experiences (Graham 1982).

Some theoretical work may be seen to have a direct and particular impact on the world at large and in other cases, there may be a more generalized seepage outwards. Much of the time, however, theoretical battles royal full of routs and reverses, may take place in academic journals and conferences without anyone outside (including some of the very subjects of the theorizing) being aware that any such thing has even gone on. This is no less true of theoretical work on disability and motherhood than anything else. This is not to denigrate theory or theorizing, it is merely to suggest that we do well to be circumspect about how widespread is the impact of any particular theoretical development.

Questioning the nature, ethics and politics of research production and whose interests are served by it, has been one element of the debates initiated by disabled academics and others who share similar theoretical perspectives (Oliver 1992; Barnes and Mercer 1997; Ward 1997). Among other things, they have raised serious questions about whether the enormously expensive research industry as it currently operates, has had much of a beneficial impact on the lives of disabled children and adults. Some have advocated an emancipatory paradigm which challenges the established power relations of research production. Oliver (1992: 111) suggests

> The issue then for the emancipatory research paradigm is not how to empower people but, once people have decided to empower themselves, precisely what research can do to facilitate this process.

He proposes that in any such enterprise, issues of gain, reciprocity and empowerment need to be interrogated.

While some might challenge Oliver's conclusion about the central issue for emancipatory research, few responsible researchers can fail to be concerned about questions about who gains from research, who has the power over what is researched, who controls the enterprise and what is the balance and degree of reciprocity that can be achieved between parties. These issues apply as much to the research undertaken for this book as to any other project. The modest steps that were taken to try to make the experience worthwhile for those who partipated will be outlined briefly in Chapter 3.

Concluding comments

A great deal has happened in policy and research on childhood disability since the mid-1970s, about the lifespan of the sons and daughters of the women who took part in the West Midlands study.

Notwithstanding the substantial developments that can be traced in research, theory and public policy across this period however, as Baldwin and Carlisle (1994) point out, there is much in the pattern of findings of research on the households of disabled children that is remarkably constant over time. Strikingly similar data emerge from studies which adopt a variety of approaches to the subject and important commonalities are evident from work which focuses on children with very different impairing conditions, living in different geographical locations and so on. It is salutary to find that recent research on mothers' experiences echoes some of the findings of investigations undertaken more than 20 years earlier. This is evident when in the next two chapters, we turn to the study of the 12 West Midlands mothers and to the broader field of research on the experience of others in a similar position.

 **2**

Twelve West Midlands mothers

The study

The study that forms part of this book was conducted in 1996. It set out to place centre stage those experiences of mothers-as-mediators. Through detailed discussions with 12 mothers, I aimed to find out what they felt was distinctive about the role played by mothers in the upbringing of their disabled sons and daughters and whether mediating activities featured significantly. I was interested in exploring what they tried to do and how and why they did it. The study focused essentially on their rationale.

In this particular case, a small-scale qualitative approach was chosen. There is already in existence a substantial body of quantitative empirical research on households of disabled children and we therefore already have access to data on the needs and circumstances of quite large-scale samples of the population. The existing empirical literature has a great deal to tell us about the lives of mothers and in addition, allows us to gauge whether the circumstances and experiences described by those in smaller samples reflect, in some respects at least, situations typical for the population as a whole. A small-scale, qualitative approach was seen to be appropriate for this piece of work because the study aimed to offer the women the opportunity to give very detailed and personal accounts of some facets of their social world. It sought their interpretations of experiences which are commonplace for them and for many other mothers of disabled children. We know from empirical studies, for example, that mothers are very active in negotiating with service providers on their disabled children's behalf (Sloper and Turner 1982). Through this study, I wished to understand how a relatively small group of women conceptualized that activity.

The mothers all lived in the West Midlands area of the UK, a region with very diverse characteristics. It has both rural and urban landscapes and populations. Parts of the region have traditionally been economically dependent on agriculture while others on heavy industry and manufacturing. There is considerable variation in prosperity from one part of the area to another with some populations experiencing severe economic decline and others relative stability. The populations of the large urban areas in particular are ethnically diverse, reflecting patterns of migration in the post-Second World War period.

The mothers had sons and daughters who were over 16 years of age and who all had sensory or physical impairments. In addition, some had learning disabilities. I chose this age group for two main reasons. First the past two decades (the lifespan of the young people concerned) have seen considerable changes in approaches to disability and services to disabled people. It was interesting to hear the experiences of women for whom disability was central to their lives across such a period. Second, I wanted to hear from women who had experienced and could reflect upon the whole span of their sons' and daughters' childhood and approaching adulthood. They had all passed through key transitional phases such as the identification of disability, accessing education and moving from children's to adult provision. I made contact with them through two main routes: a national college of further education for people with physical and sensory impairments and a network of parents who in the early 1980s, had been active in campaigning for inclusive education for their then young children.

The college draws its students from the whole of the UK and in a small number of cases, from other countries. Some of its facilities are highly specialized in that they cater for students whose complex learning and support needs cannot at this point be met appropriately in their local further education colleges. The college's programmes of further and higher education are, however, open to local disabled students whose needs are less complex and to those who are non-disabled.

The college wrote a letter about the project to all students' mothers who lived in the West Midlands and whose sons or daughters were over 16 years of age and were living with physical or sensory impairments. Of the 17 contacted, nine agreed to participate. In addition, one mother whose son was not yet at college heard of the project from others and asked to be included. As she and her son met all the criteria, her participation was welcomed.

Because the college caters for some students with very complex learning and support needs, it seemed likely, given their ages and policy on inclusion in the recent past, that most would have received their education outside the mainstream sector. In order to ensure that the experience of some mothers whose children had gone to mainstream school was included in the project, I made contact with the woman who had been secretary of the committee of a network of parents who had campaigned for inclusive education in the early 1980s. There had been six mothers on the original committee and the secretary knew of the whereabouts of only three. One of those lived outside the West Midlands. The two remaining agreed to participate in the project.

In the initial contact stage, all the women were asked to specify their preferred language for future discussion and communication so that interpreting and translating could be arranged where appropriate.

I contacted all the women for a preliminary discussion about the project in order to give them the chance to ask questions and to give some thought in advance to what they might like to discuss in the main interview. Seven of these preliminary discussions took place by telephone and three face-to-face. For one of the mothers, this and all future contact was conducted with the aid of an interpreter.

In this preliminary exchange, I explained that I was interested in their views alone and that I would like to talk with them about what they felt was distinctive about the things that mothers of disabled children had to do. I emphasized that I would find it interesting and important to hear about the things that they perhaps regarded as ordinary and unremarkable because they were part and parcel of their lives. I also said that I would like to hear from their point of view, whether they found themselves involved in negotiation, mediation or explaining work with their disabled child or with others on the child's behalf. All the women used the opportunity to check out that they understood the focus of the project. They gave examples that readily sprang to mind and asked if that was the sort of thing that I would be interested in hearing about.

All interviews took place in the women's own homes and lasted between one and a half and three hours. Ten were tape-recorded and in two, at the mothers' request, I took written notes. The interviews were structured only insofar as I had determined the three key areas for discussion: the particular role of mothers; explaining work with their sons and daughters; negotiating and mediating with other people. Following the interviews, contact was maintained in order to give the mothers information about the outcome of the project and plans for publication.

The majority of the women expressed a great deal of interest and curiosity in the project and liked the idea of a study which listened to mothers' versions of their lives and recognized and respected their contribution. When the interviews were completed, most volunteered that that they had enjoyed the experience or found it interesting. The majority also said that their motivation for taking part was that they wanted to pass on their experience in the hope that it would benefit someone else directly or indirectly. They liked the fact that their ideas were to be included in a book which might be read by exist- ing professionals and those in training and could possibly have some influence on their perceptions. While they were not overoptimistic about the impact that their ideas might have, the majority took the view that 'you never know' or 'every little helps'.

I did not pay the women concerned for the interviews with them but it was possible to come to an agreement, with those who wished, that I would do something in return for them. In a small sample such as this, it is not too difficult to find modest but practical and appropriate ways of reciprocating. For example, some needed information that they found difficult to track down, some who spent their lives cooking for others liked the idea of going out for a meal, others wanted assistance to access a service. One woman said that her main motivation for taking part was that she felt the need to talk about painful experiences that had happened more than 20 years before and which still hurt her. She said that the interview itself was helpful but she also asked me to research the range of counselling services in her area so that she could have the option of seeking help.

I made contact with the women and had my meetings with them in the spring of 1996. The thumbnail sketches of them and their circumstances outlined here are based on information that they gave at that time. All of them chose pseudonyms for themselves and other members of their families. In the intervening two years since meeting the women and completing the book, however, things have changed dramatically and sadly in two of the households. Both Margaret and Jean have died and Jean's son, Robert, also died within a short time of his mother. I have not changed the pen pictures of them that were written at the time I met them because they give a flavour of the lives of the two women who spoke the words that contributed so much to this part of the book. The rest of the chapter describes the women briefly and gives their accounts of their experiences as mothers and mediators in the last two decades.

The women and their circumstances

Deborah lives with her husband Gary, her son Simon, and her daughter Catherine in a small, prosperous dormitory town near a city. Deborah is a part-time library assistant and her husband works in the Post Office. Simon is away at university during term time. Catherine is 25 and lives at home. She attends a specialist further education college as a day student. She has cerebral palsy resulting in mobility and speech difficulties. Deborah is white and was born in the UK.

Vera also described her ethnic background as 'white UK'. Her husband, who is a manual worker, came from Ireland as a young man to work in the large city where she was born. They have lived there throughout their marriage. They have five children. Matthew, the youngest at 16, has cerebral palsy and attends a specialist further education college as a residential student. He comes home to his parents in the holidays and for some weekends. Vera's other sons and daughter have their own homes and live locally. Vera has a part-time job as a cleaner now that Matthew is at college.

Mary described herself as 'white working class, married to somebody Scottish'. She lives in a village in a rural area. She works part-time in a nursing home for older people. She has had no formal training since leaving school and says that she has always seen bringing up the children as her forte. She has two sons: Steve, 20, and Richard, 15. Steve has spina bifida and hydrocephalus and attends the specialist further education college as a day student. Mary's husband is a white-collar worker and has what she describes as 'a good job'.

Fazialt Jan lives in an industrial area of a large city with her husband, a factory worker and her daughter Shamim. Shamim is 24 and has learning difficulties and physical impairments resulting from spina bifida and hydrocephalus. She attends the specialist college as a day student. Fazialt Jan's other son and daughter are both married and living away from home. Fazialt Jan was born in Pakistan and her mother tongue is Urdu. She speaks little English.

Jean has become disabled over recent years as a result of the onset of a painful arthritic condition. She and her husband, Bill, live with their son Rob in a suburban area of a large city. Rob is 20 years of age. In addition to his learning difficulties, he has a serious heart condition, has survived a stroke and has other related health problems. He attends the specialist college of further education as a day student. Bill was a skilled manual worker who was made redundant two years ago. In recent times, as Jean's impairments have increased, Bill has become more involved in caring tasks for which Jean had previously taken responsibility.

Margaret is a physiotherapist and has two children: William, 17 and Carol, 13. William has congenital rubella syndrome and is at a residential school during the week. Margaret and her husband, Jim, live in a suburb of a large city. They are white and born in the United Kingdom.

Angela also lives in a suburb of a large city with her husband and five daughters. Her second daughter, Louise, age 24, has cerebral palsy which affects her mobility and speech. Louise attends the specialist college on a daily basis. Angela does not have a job outside the home. Her husband is a skilled manual worker. They are white and born in the UK.

Destiny is of South Asian origin and she has three children whom she has brought up alone. Her eldest son, Nik, 18, has Duechenne muscular dystrophy. At the time of our meeting, Nik's condition was quite advanced and he was described as being very seriously ill. When he feels well enough, Destiny takes him by car to the specialist college of further education where he still does a small number of sessions. Destiny works as a driver and lives in a small town in a country area.

Elaine is a nurse who works in a nursing home for older people. Before she had her children, she was a nurse in a hospital for children with multiple and profound impairments. She lives in a market town in a country area with her two children, Jonathan, 18, and Elizabeth, 13. The other member of the household is Kevin, Jonathan's stepfather, who has been together with her since Jonathan was 18 months old. Both Jon and Elizabeth have cerebral palsy. Jon has a residential place at the specialist college of further education. Everyone in the household is white and from the United Kingdom.

Victoria lives in a suburb of a city and is a secretary and clerical worker. She is married to David, a skilled worker, and has two children: Louisa, age 20 and Paul, age 17. Paul, who has cerebral palsy, attends a local college of further education. All members of the household were born in the United Kingdom and are white.

Ann is a teacher who also lives in a suburban area of a large city where she was born. She is white and lives with her son, John, 18, who became disabled as a result of having a spinal tumour when he was young. John attends a local college of further education. Ann's husband, Dave, who was also disabled, died two years ago.

Jane is also a white, lone mother who lives in a suburb of a large city. She works part-time as a secretary and receptionist. Her son Phil, who is 18, sustained brain injury following a road traffic accident at the age of 9 years. Some time after Phil's accident, Jane began to train as a teacher. She had to give up university, however, as she found that she could not manage her course work as well as offering Phil the care and support he needed. Phil now attends the specialist college as a residential student.

On being a mother

There was a great deal of common ground among the women who took part in the study about the things that distinguished the role of mothers from those played by significant others in the child's or young person's life. Both from their own personal experience and from their observations of the lives of others in a similar position, it was their overwhelming view that in most households it tended to be mothers who had the central responsibility for the care and upbringing of disabled children and young adults. While they acknowledged the contribution made by other members of their households, they were quite clear that it mainly fell to them to provide the direct and ongoing personal care, support and assistance. They were also the ones who took most responsibility for keeping track, organizing and making sure that things happened as well as taking on the majority of dealings with outside professionals and their organizations. If something new needed to be done or if an existing arrangement came unstuck, it was the mothers who extended themselves either to absorb the task personally or to sort something out. In addition, some felt that mothers tended to deal with emotional issues and situations where there was a question of feelings needing to be sorted out within their households and extended families. In one form or another, mediation, interpretation and shuttle diplomacy figured repeatedly in their descriptions of what they, as mothers, were required to do at a variety of levels and in a range of circumstances.

Very quickly the situation of their having most responsibility became self-reinforcing. By virtue of undertaking all of these tasks, the mothers became

the adults who had the most knowledge of what needed to be done and therefore continued to do it. Not only did the women assume a central role in relation to this set of essential activities, but such was the nature of this work that
it in turn had a fundamental and ongoing impact which structured their lives.
Margaret summarized her views in this way:

> I think that mothers take a pivotal position with any child. I think it's the
> same with your able-bodied child, but they of course require a lot less of
> the sort of go-between activity, except when they're young. But if I look
> at friends I've made who have all got disabled children, with the odd
> exception, the mother is the one who will take them where they need to
> go. You know, if you've got hospital appointments and if you've got a
> severely disabled child, you may have three, four or five consultants to
> go and see. It's not possible if fathers are working, to have time off and so
> you tend to be the one that goes and does it all. You tend to be the one
> to make the phone calls to people, you take them to school, you liaise
> with teachers. Also because you've grown up with the child and you
> have them all the time, you know them . . . their ins and outs and all the
> different things probably better than the father however much involved
> they are . . . You're always alert, reading the signs . . . In fact the only
> time I'm off duty is when Will's not there!

She went on to point out the time-consuming and all-encompassing nature
of the work:

> Everybody comes in. I mean, when they're little you feel as if you've got
> open house. You know, three or four times a week somebody, some pro-
> fessional, might come in. And that is very difficult and I don't think they
> always realize but they are actually invading your home.

Ann also saw the fact that her partner had had a paid job while she stayed
at home as being a major factor in determining who did what when their disabled son was young.

> You're available more than anybody else. You're the ones who take them
> to the hospital and it's mostly you that speaks to the professionals . . . and
> it's mostly you that faces people.

Jane had similar views about how the division of labour came about and
was concerned about some of the consequences for the women when such
arrangements became established.

> Among the mums I've spoken to, even when they have got a partner, the
> partner tends to go out to work and be the breadwinner and then the
> mother's trying to juggle. You know, a lot can't work again once they've
> got a disabled child and so they're really trapped. It's very difficult.

While much agreement emerged among the women in the study about what
was distinctive about the things that mothers did, there were also variations in
their experience. These included matters related to their material circumstances

and supportive relationships as well as the health status of adults within their households.

Mary, Victoria and Ann pointed out that not having to worry about money all the time made a difference to theirs and their sons' lives. None of them saw themselves as well off but they had enough material resources to allow themselves and their children a wider range of choices and room for manoeuvre. When families had a little extra money, they could manage to pay for something that really worked for their child or which was not readily provided by state services. The young person might, for example, have driving lessons earlier and be able to consider a car of their own as an immediate and attainable goal. This might in turn, have repercussions for the degree of independence that mothers and children could expect to have from each other. Those such as Fazialt Jan and Vera, who did not have much to spare, were up against greater restrictions and a smaller range of choices.

The majority of those living with partners were appreciative of their contribution but nevertheless saw themselves as carrying the central, ongoing responsibility. Their partners tended to undertake practical jobs, physical tasks or leisure activities or to become involved for particular reasons if the occasion seemed to demand it. Mary had this to say:

> I'm lucky with my husband because he's very good with children and I know a lot of men aren't . . . But at the end of the day a lot of it is left to me even though I'm lucky because my husband takes some of the strain off me . . . The hygiene and all that sort of thing is left to me but he does things like helping Steve in and out of the bath . . . he's extremely good that way.

Angela also said that her husband helped a great deal but that she automatically saw most things as her job to do, particularly when it came to providing intimate and personal care for her daughter. Angela was reluctant to ask her other daughters to step in unless they actively volunteered. They all placed a high value, she said, on the closeness of their family and she did not want to risk any resentment on the part of Louise's sisters by asking too much of them. A workable balance had to be struck.

Victoria, like some of the other women, said that she had done 'most of the running about to appointments and so on' and that her husband had mainly become involved with professionals and their organizations when they found that they had a fight on their hands over crucial decisions about education. Other women, too, gave examples of their partners taking time to go to meetings or appointments that were regarded as very significant or potentially difficult. Ann called it 'being shipped in for the biggies'.

Some of the women highlighted further ways in which their own and their male partners' roles differed. Victoria talked in some detail about the fact that she believed that women were more likely than men to deal with issues or situations that were related to emotions. They also tended to take responsibility for trying to solve problems which involved close personal relationships in some way. Victoria said of fathers:

I don't think that it's that they don't want to be involved . . . As far as David's concerned, give him something practical to do – the gaiters on the legs and so on – and he's fully involved. I think he's fairly typical . . . They have a different view of it. It's not their fault. Nobody blames them for it. It's just the way things are.

Three other women had also come to similar conclusions. When it came to dealing with matters which had 'emotional overtones' Margaret said:

I think it's always going to fall to somebody in any relationship. Certainly in our relationship if Jim can get away without explaining anything like that, he will . . . Again, that is his nature . . . and he wouldn't have the words. Like a lot of men he can't express feelings. He's great but he deals with facts!

While Ann had been a lone mother for the two years since the death of Dave, her partner, she frequently referred to the time when she was in a two-parent household, a period that made up the majority of her son's childhood. She and her partner had divided the tasks to be done in the way already described by most women in the study. Ann, however, felt that her approach was enhanced and supported by Dave in a very singular and important way. His own experience of being disabled gave him great confidence in sorting out the wheat from the chaff as far as service provision was concerned and also demystified a lot of issues for Ann. She said this:

Dave was very practical about the whole thing and he took everything with a pinch of salt because he'd got so much more experience of the whole set-up than I had and he also knew how to manage his own disability. He was a lot more dismissive of all sorts of things than I dared be because he'd taken risks himself . . . If he thought something was totally pointless, he didn't feel he had to go along with it . . . I never thought of Dave as disabled, you see, not in the usual sense and I don't think he did either. He just had this illness that had to be dealt with.

Jean's position was rather different from the others whose partners helped out. Until recent years, she too had taken central responsibility for providing the care and attention that Robert needed. Her husband's role had been important but less pivotal than her own. Redundancy from his job two years before, however, had coincided with the worsening of Jean's arthritic condition and since then, there had been significant changes in the nature and balance of the work that they undertook respectively in relation to Rob. Bill had recently taken on many of the tasks and responsibilities hitherto accomplished or managed by Jean. After so many years of responsibility, she saw this change as no less upsetting for being inevitable, saying:

When he was made redundant, I was made redundant as well because he took over. Not nasty nor nothing like that. That was just how it had to be. He just had to take over and do it all.

Two of the women, Fazialt Jan and Vera, who had partners living with them said that they alone were responsible for all aspects of the care and assistance their daughter and son needed. Their husbands' involvement was seen as very limited. Fazialt Jan said that her husband did not do anything to help with Shamim and that there was no one else in the household to give her assistance. In a largely unadapted house, all tasks, including the ones that required physical strength such as carrying her daughter upstairs, fell to her. While she did not expect or want her husband to assist with their daughter's personal care, Fazialt Jan felt generally unsupported within her household and wider family. She also felt very isolated and cut off from other basic forms of help, contact and association which she felt would benefit her daughter and herself.

Vera, also quite isolated, had this to say of mothers, fathers and her own situation:

> Mothers have to bring them up more than fathers because the fathers are at work all day. He's too tired when he comes home, so it's really all down to the mothers. I've done everything for Matthew, even bathed him before we had the shower put in last year. I've done the lot . . . We're close and he's not so close to his dad. Mothers and their kids are different to fathers and their kids . . . Kids rely on their mothers more than their fathers.

For the three women who did not have a partner living with them, the question of shared responsibility for any aspect of care and assistance did not arise.

Ann missed Dave and the contribution that he had made to John's life and her own. As John grew older, there were some discussions that she had had with him, for example about sexual development, which she as a woman and his mother, felt could have been difficult. It was not that she was unwilling to talk with him or that she felt that things had gone badly, but rather that she would have preferred him to have the choice of discussing such intimate things with a man. In the main, however, she felt that she and John got on very well. She viewed her son as a bright and independent young man whom she did not see as making unreasonable demands upon her.

Jane and Destiny, the other lone mothers, described circumstances which were at times at least, exceptionally taxing. Although Jane felt more supported by her extended family than Destiny, both felt that the responsibility for giving their sons the high levels of assistance, care and support that they needed fell entirely to them. The giving of this care sometimes felt all-consuming. Jane described what happened after Phil's accident:

> I just think there's not very much care in the community as such. When Phil was discharged from hospital, there wasn't any back-up at all apart from what I had with my family and that tended to get less and less. I was sort of left to it, if you see what I mean. I had one particular sister who was very good. She used to come round after school. She's a teacher. But

I found that the others had got their own families and it was difficult for them. I mean you can't expect people to drop everything. So more and more is taken on by myself as mum and you know, there wasn't anybody else to turn to. You just had to get on with it basically. I became very worn out but there wasn't much help at all.

She went on to describe how she took sole responsibility for the next nine years:

Things were very difficult and I think that you're always worrying that you're doing the right thing because as a single parent you haven't got anybody to discuss that many things with . . . You were the one that did the majority of it and when you closed the door at night you were on your own. You just tend to live from day to day and you hope that life's going to get . . . that there's going to be light at the end of the tunnel . . . Then there was the sheer loneliness of it all. I feel the worst part was the loneliness really. Phil would be in bed at night and I'd always be stuck in. If I wanted to go anywhere I'd have to get someone to look after him and nine times out of ten I couldn't.

Destiny also did not feel that she had anyone able to help her in what were extremely harrowing circumstances. At the time of our discussion, she said that her son's health was extremely fragile and that she did not expect him to survive very far into adulthood. For a number of years she had been the person giving him the high levels of support and care that he required and her previous negative experience of services and professionals left her reluctant to trust intervention by others at this critical time. As a lone mother with two other children and little other adult help, her life seemed to have been exceptionally demanding in recent years. She described herself as often feeling 'exhausted', 'frightened' and 'isolated' and she said this:

We live a very sheltered life. I have to assist him in every way. I live for Nik and my life is completely full, day and night. Our lives are so intertwined. As his mother, you're put in this position whether you want to be or not.

To some degree, the particular mothering activities that the women undertook in relation to their disabled children were seen as a logical or inevitable extension of the more general mothering roles and activities that others expected of them and that they, in part at least, expected of themselves. In considering how this was determined, they pointed to traditional divisions of labour which exist between men and women generally both inside and outside the home, to the structural and practical arrangements in their lives which had both grown out of and reinforced such divisions, to attributes that they identified as being more usually associated with men or women and to the characteristics and inclinations of the individual adults and children concerned.

So while the mothers described the distinctive features of their relationships with and arrangements for their disabled children, the majority were also at pains to draw parallels with the upbringing and support needed by all children, including others in their own families. As mothers, they were trying to operate on the same or similar sets of principles but with added dimensions to take into account the needs of their disabled child. Those dimensions and the particular circumstances in which some found themselves, however, often made extraordinary demands upon them, demands which went far beyond those that many mothers would routinely expect to have to meet.

Mediation

In some form or another, mediation was a live issue for all of the women. One of the many striking features of the discussions with them was the degree of modesty that they displayed when they described their often quite complex mediating activities. While they expressed emotion and conviction about all sorts of subjects and experiences, they were often very matter-of-fact about the detail of their mediating work, projecting it as simply what they did because it needed doing.

For those young people whose speech could not readily be understood by others, the women were often literally their interpreters. The women also described how they interceded in a host of other ways between their disabled son or daughter and people and circumstances that fostered misunderstanding of them and their needs. Their intimate relationships with their children gave them an understanding and a commitment that they felt often flew in the face of the assumptions they met about disabled children in general and their children in particular. They therefore mediated between their disabled children and other people, manoeuvred within an often limited space, to bring about what they regarded as achievable changes. Sometimes the achievable change was practical or material. At other times they were concerned to change hearts and minds. At the same time as trying to bring about changes in others, they also encouraged their disabled children to see things in ways that would stand them in good stead. Sometimes that meant helping them to have a view that was different from the dominant received wisdom.

Angela said that it was a family joke that with the practice she had had at negotiation, she could get a job at the United Nations. Margaret spoke of 'always trying to redress the balance'. Deborah's view of it was this:

> You are constantly presenting an alternative image of your child to the outside world . . . You are constantly changing their minds.

While mediation was an important and ongoing feature in all their lives, there was variation among the women over where they focused most of their energies and the sites where they undertook most activity. Their experiences, however, fell into four main groups: dealings with family and friends, encounters in public places, negotiations with services and work directly with their disabled children.

Dealing with family and friends

Seven of the women in the study who had more than one child felt that they had to intercede between their disabled child and others in the household. They had a strong sense that it was important to increase their non-disabled children's awareness and understanding but believed it was a fine line between that and asking too much of them. Attempting to avoid resentment or jealousy through discussion with non disabled children was raised as an important issue by five of the women.

Angela put great store by showing that everyone was treated fairly:

> I think it helps if you try to look at it from the point of view of balancing the family out . . . You have to be so careful with them growing up that there's no resentment. They need to see that she's treated equally and that she's not favoured because she's handicapped . . . It's important for Emily being younger. If she saw Louise doing something that she knew was wrong and she was allowed to do it, it could build up resentment.

Angela felt that it was also important to enhance Emily's understanding of her elder sister's situation and to do this in a way that was respectful to Louise:

> I rely a lot on discussing and explaining things really . . . Sometimes Emily says to me, 'If I'd done that, you'd have been angry with me.' I say to her, 'You have to stop and think how Louise's life is compared with yours. She can't just get up and do something like you can. So she gets angry because she wants to do it and this builds up and she has a major tantrum' . . . They do accept it. They're incredible really but on the other hand I have to be careful not to emphasize it too much. I have to make Emily realize what Louise's situation is without dramatizing it too much and worrying her or making her feel bad.

Victoria spoke of what happened with her non-disabled daughter when she and her husband were spending a great deal of time and energy on the formal procedures needed to get their disabled son into mainstream school:

> It was tough. All your energies seem to go on one child and I think Louisa missed out a bit at that time. She says now she remembers and she resented all the attention. She saw it as attention, you see, which is quite a natural instinct as a child. So when I realized, I asked her if she was happy with the life she'd got and how she was going to school and stuff like that and she said, 'Yes', and I explained that that was all we wanted for her brother as well and that was what it was all about. At the time she seemed happy with the explanation. I think it was enough at that point.

Although Destiny said that she tried to explain as much as possible to her younger children and to give them the attention they needed, she expressed great concern about whether in their present circumstances, she could meet everyone's needs.

Jean also said that it had not been possible to overcome the jealousy felt by the children of her first marriage towards their disabled stepbrother and that this had persisted into adult life. She felt that these days both she and Rob were pitied by one of her daughters, a sentiment that she found demeaning. She said:

> I don't need you to feel sorry . . . There's a difference between saying life is hard for somebody in some ways and feeling pity, isn't there? There's a very big distinction between that.

Margaret explained that she hoped that at some future time, it might be possible for her disabled son to live independently of his family in an appropriate supported living scheme. It therefore came as a shock to her to realize that Carol, her younger daughter, by the age of 10, had begun to see herself as having future caring responsibilities for her elder brother. Margaret felt it important to give her a different view not only of her own life but of opportunities her brother might have:

> She just actually said very openly,'When you and dad aren't here, I'll be responsible for him'. Now that is something that makes you, as a mother, sit back. It wasn't that she said, 'Will I?' it was just, 'I will be'. And I sort of said, 'No. You won't be. I want you always to take an interest in Will and perhaps to make sure he's in the right place, but you'll never be responsible for him . . . But you know, if you got married, had a family, had children, I'd like your children to know Uncle William and you could perhaps invite him over for a meal and that sort of thing'.

Sometimes brothers and sisters of a disabled child needed explanations or suggestions when they came across situations outside the family that made them feel uncomfortable or at a loss. Several mothers said that children who themselves were at ease with their disabled brother or sister, found it difficult when they came in contact with someone whom they felt was awkward or had the wrong attitude. Sometimes they took that person on directly themselves and came to their mothers later for a debriefing. At other times, mothers intervened to support them, explain or make suggestions.

Mary talked about her younger son, Richard, becoming upset at the age of 7 when they were on holiday abroad in a place where there were few wheelchair users out and about other than his brother. People stared openly at Steve and Richard became distressed and very protective towards him.

> It was the first time that Richard really became aware of other people's reactions to Steve. I explained to him, 'You know yourself that Steve's fine and you're happy with him. A lot of people aren't rude. Most people are nice . . . Some just don't understand'. I mean, how do you explain to a 7 year old? But I think he accepted it and felt better after that.

Angela's younger daughter, Emily, had been upset because some of her friends had been reluctant to come and play in the house because they had no experience of mixing with a young disabled adult like her sister, Louise. Angela had explained to Emily that the best thing was to go out of her way to show them how to behave. She should talk to Louise in the way that she normally did and have the usual jokes with her. The friends who probably did not know what to do, would then be more likely to follow her lead and become used to the situation.

Most of the mothers and their children had contact of some sort with extended family and there was a consensus that if possible, these were important relationships to maintain. Family could not be ignored or rejected without some, often substantial, personal costs for all concerned. Most of the women did not wish that to happen. They often made considerable efforts to ensure that relationships were kept on an even keel. This was sometimes not easy if they felt that a relative's attitude or behaviour towards their disabled child needed to be modified or challenged in some way. The inevitability of contact, however, meant that something usually had to be sorted out one way or another.

Margaret said that she had some good, supportive relationships with relatives, particularly perhaps with her mother-in-law. She pointed out, however, that discussing things to do with her disabled son with people in her extended family, particularly those like her mother to whom she had been very close, sometimes proved more difficult than talking to acquaintances or strangers. The other emotions, roles and relationships of obligation that were involved within families could make it difficult for her to get her message across and for it to be heard. She had sometimes even gone to the lengths of practising something new or upsetting on an acquaintance first in order to be sure that she could then tell her family without becoming 'too emotional'. If she became too emotional, she said, the family would only hear her upset and the essential message that she was trying to get across about William would be lost.

Five of the women spoke of a variety of issues that they had had to tackle with different family members who had little experience of disabled people. Two had had fairly strong reactions from people who regarded disability as a stigma and felt that disabled people should be hidden away. In Jean's case, despite trying to maintain contact in the first 18 months of her son's life, her relationship with her parents-in-law had broken down irrevocably because they believed that Rob should have been placed in an institution. Others mentioned awkwardness with older family members who, it was suggested, had been brought up at a time when disability was not mentioned or was swept under the carpet.

Elaine's father did not regard disability as a stigma but simply could not accept that Jonathan was disabled. Consequently, he was always telling his grandson that he would 'get better'. Elaine said:

> I had to talk to my dad myself . . . I had to explain to him that he just had to accept it. He kept telling Jon that he'd be walking next year and playing football, building up his hopes . . . not being honest.

Deborah felt that one of her uncles had adopted an extremely patronizing attitude to Catherine and had assumed that ordinary aspirations about work and lifestyle would be beyond her. She felt that she found an effective way of challenging this and getting her own back a little without upsetting things too much. Catherine wrote poetry and when she had her first poem published, Deborah had a copy made into a Christmas card that she sent to the uncle. She said:

> I suppose I was indulging myself a bit . . . saying 'So there!' but he'd made me so cross . . . I forget the term he used but he'd obviously written her off as a burden to us . . . a shame . . . a 'what are you going to do with her' sort of thing.

Three of the women gave examples of having to intercede routinely and tactfully over fairly small-scale incidents when a relative was trying to do something positive but inappropriate. Someone might be overindulgent, too enthusiastic with help or assistance or might undermine the young person by paying too much attention to them or treating them as a much younger child.

The situation with friends was a little different. Friendship could all too easily fall away when people were uncomfortable with disabled children, their parents and the circumstances surrounding them. Seven of the mothers volunteered some experience of this. Fazialt Jan said quite simply:

> If my family doesn't care, how can I expect people outside of my family to care?

After Phil's accident, Jane also was very hurt by the reaction of some of her own and her son's friends:

> And friends, you know that Phil had before the accident, well they didn't know how to deal with it and they would rather cross over the road rather than talk to him. And that hurt me . . . At first when he was start-ing on the road to recovery . . . we used to have an ambulance that picked him up from outside the house . . . people, friends, would walk past and look the other way and I used to feel like screaming out at them, you know, 'Why don't you just talk to us? Why don't you just come and say hello?' Sometimes people would talk to me and not to him as if he didn't exist . . . because he was obviously disabled. I felt that they were too embarrassed to talk to him because they felt that he wouldn't be able to communicate or wouldn't understand what they were saying. It used to hurt Phil and he used to get very frustrated about it. Sometimes, he'd just walk off.

Jane tried a number of tactics to improve the situation, including inviting other children home, offering people a lead by the way she spoke and behaved to Phil and by asking Phil's scoutmaster to help bridge the gap between him and the other boys. She said that a lot of the time her efforts proved in vain. In the early days, when someone did, unusually, follow her lead and get involved in con-versation with Phil, she found herself feeling grateful to them, a reaction that she felt was sad somehow. Things had, however, improved in this respect since he had been at college, progress which she regarded as extremely important.

Jean had had experience of her son when younger, becoming very distressed because other children had taunted and made fun of him. Like Jane, she had invited the children to play in an effort to break down barriers.

Margaret said that she had good friends and that she thought carefully about how many demands to make on them. She thought that becoming someone who talked only of problems was the surest way to lose them. If there was a time when things were difficult with Will, she thought it important to acknowledge this with friends and she sometimes tried to do so in general terms that might strike a chord. She would speak of 'teenage problems' or 'sorting a few things out with the school'. Because she was also aware that people had a tendency to stereotype disabled people exclusively as problems, she did not want to feed into that. In fact, she said, she spent a lot of time presenting an alternative image which she felt was nearer reality but contrary to the dominant view held by others.

Others, too, had valued friendships with people who were accepting of all family members and their lifestyle. There was particular appreciation of people who did ordinary things with their sons and daughters without making too much of it or those who changed their attitudes about something important. Jean spoke of one such family friend who had initially assumed that her son could not have any sexual feelings:

> He said to me, 'What does Rob want for Christmas?' And I said, 'He wants a *Baywatch*, a Pamela Anderson calendar.' He said, 'You what? You're joking!' I said, 'No I'm not. Why shouldn't he?' And this is from a bloke who's known him most of his life. It's because he's mentally handicapped, you see, and people don't expect it. They don't expect him to think like that. Anyway, in the end, the bloke said, 'Yeah. Why shouldn't he?' So he got his Pamela Anderson calendar.

Encounters in public places

The majority of the women were of the view that public attitudes towards disabled people had improved and that the built environment also had fewer barriers than before. Most were also equally emphatic that there was still a very long way to go.

Frequently, when they were with their sons and daughters in public places, things happened that were not to their liking. They then felt that they had the responsibility to manage the situation in some way. They had to make a decision on the spot about whether this was something to be challenged or allowed to drop. If they decided not to let the matter drop, they had to decide quickly what was the best course of action. In coming to their conclusions, they took a range of personal and situational factors into account. One of these factors was what they believed their son or daughter might feel and what they might regard as the most positive or least detrimental course of action.

More than half of the women expressed anger about the way their sons and daughters could be excluded from doing the things that other people took for granted because of access problems in public places. Over the years, some had become more demanding about decent access and less tolerant about assumptions that their children should fit in with an unsuitable environment.

Vera said that she used to apologize for the amount of space Matthew's wheelchair took up on pavements and elsewhere but that she had begun to have a different view. She had noticed that other people did not look where they were going and did not expect to have to make any concessions to the wheelchair and the young person in it. She said that consequently she had long since stopped apologizing despite the fact that people got 'uptight'. She added that she thought it awful that Matthew should still often have to wait outside a building simply because there was no wheelchair access. She felt that this dented his confidence and made him reluctant to go out independently of her in case he should come across a barrier that could not be overcome without help.

Victoria did not hide her feelings:

> I've been banging the drum forever about things like ramps! You know, I'd walk round town and I'd say, 'For Christ's sake! It's a disgrace!' It's a nightmare . . . not just here but everywhere . . . parking for disabled people's appalling.

She said that she had often been very outspoken in public. Sometimes her son had approved of his mother's behaviour and sometimes he had said, 'For God's sake, leave it out!'.

Elaine said that in relation to the built environment it was important to let it be known where the fault lay. Otherwise children might blame themselves when they could not get in somewhere. When they had had to leave a swimming pool because Jonathan could not gain access, she pointed out quite clearly that the problem was theirs not his.

The women in the study also described, however, how they made compromises or avoided unnecessary battles, particularly if in their judgement, the gains to be made were outweighed by the losses. Margaret described how her 17 year old son's loud 'screeching' had made the whole of the Asda supermarket fall silent. She expected some leeway from other shoppers but on the occasions that she judged Will's behaviour to be too demanding, she would decide that discretion was the better part of valour and head for the nearest exit. She also talked about strategies for increasing to a degree she regarded as reasonable, people's tolerance of Will's unexpected and challenging behaviour in social situations. She described the scene in a restaurant where she feared people could react badly:

> If it happens in a restaurant, for instance, that's slightly more difficult because you're in an area where people expect to have quiet and have gone for a quiet evening or a more refined atmosphere . . . And if somebody starts creating, then it is more difficult and tolerance may be less . . . I don't know what you'll think of this but when Will does something or

is behaving badly, it's not obvious that he's deaf . . . And because he does understand a few signs, I always sign to him in those circumstances . . . We do sign to him sometimes and so he doesn't see it as an unnatural reaction . . . but really I sign to him at that point . . . not really for him but because you're saying to the world, 'Look! He can't hear. So he doesn't know he's just made that noise'. You're presenting him to the world in a different way. You're saying, 'This is his ability or disability whichever way you like to look at it, so this episode cannot be taken at face value' . . . People must be allowed within reason to be undisturbed but having said that, there's no reason why Will shouldn't participate in that sort of social event, too.

Some of the most difficult moments to manage were those where a stranger or someone only slightly known, made an approach in public that was not actively intended to be hostile but was often experienced by the disabled young people and their mothers as inappropriate or undermining. It was not unusual for mothers and children to get a stong whiff of charity in these encounters. Sometimes it also seemed that being disabled automatically made you public property and gave you a public persona that was not always welcome. Deborah explained:

Elizabeth gets annoyed when she goes into town because everyone knows her or knows of her. She can't go anywhere without someone seeing her and asking her what she's doing now . . . She's always 'the little handicapped girl' as far as people are concerned . . . but sometimes she'd just like to blend in.

Mary gave examples of 'the usual story', occasions when in her son's presence, people spoke to her about his needs and preferences as opposed to asking him directly. She felt that on the whole there were probably more good than bad people in the world and that individuals did these things merely because they had no experience and did not know how to react. She felt somewhat less forgiving, however, about the occasions when strangers had spoken to her in Steve's presence in a quiet and pitying voice, telling her that they so admired her. She did not like the way that this not only undermined her son but also characterized her as a 'saint'. Her reaction was: 'As far as I'm concerned, he's my son and that's it!'

Elaine became tired of some approaches:

It gets on my nerves when people ask me how he's getting on instead of talking to him directly . . . I say, 'Why don't you ask him?' . . . Children generally are OK . . . It's because they've been brought up more with disability now on the television and in mainstream schools. But their parents can be very prejudiced and ignorant. They think that everybody in a wheelchair's incapable and that they don't have minds of their own.

Sometimes mothers found it a dilemma when people who themselves seemed vulnerable or who 'meant well', did something that was difficult for the disabled young person. The women did not want to be too harsh but neither did they wish to collude with attitudes or actions that were degrading to their children. Angela told the story of how in a shop, a rather frail older man had approached her daughter who was in her wheelchair and had pressed a pound coin into her hand:

> That was difficult because she was really taken aback. She didn't know what to do. It was difficult because he was trying to be kind but at the same time it was because he felt sorry for her . . . I think I let it ride at the time purely out of politeness and then I spoke to Louise about it later at home.

If the women felt that the person approaching their son or daughter was genuinely well-meaning, they sometimes tried to save the situation by, themselves, behaving in an obviously different way towards the child or young person. The message was partly for the stranger and partly for the child.

Sometimes, however, by no stretch of the imagination could the approach of a stranger be regarded as benign but misguided. Jean gave a number of examples of hurtful incidents.

> And one day in town there was something going on and there was this girl giving away balloons and stuff and I was stood with Rob in his buggy . . . and there was this lady and her daughter and two grandchildren. And this girl came over with the balloons and she didn't have very many left. And this lady grabbed them all and the girl said, 'I was giving one to the little lad'. Well this woman said, 'What does he want one for? He won't know any difference'. And I said, 'I beg your pardon!' And she said, 'Well, the handicap. He won't know the difference, will he?'

Jean said that she did not feel the need to pull her punches at such times nor on the occasions when other parents deliberately moved their children to the other side of the pavement as she and her small son walked towards them. She said that her response to this was, 'It's all right. You can't catch mental handicap, you know!' Jean also said that in the face of attitudes such as these, it was difficult not to react by trying at times to prove your child and by having higher expectations of their behaviour in public than was the case with non-disabled children.

Dealing with services

The mediation that they had undertaken in relation to health, education and social service provision was a prominent and live issue for every one of the women. Each of the mothers had had experience of having to intercede in crucial ways in order to ensure that their children's needs were met.

For a number of the women, it was ironical that contact with the services that were ostensibly there to help them and their children had proved to be some of the most stressful and difficult experiences that they had had. Deborah, for example, described going to hospitals and clinics as 'a great trauma in itself rather than a help' and said that she had had to get herself 'geared up' before each visit. Even when mothers had met with success in negotiations, they found the processes involved very anxiety-provoking at some point.

At the beginning they had expected to be able to rely on the expertise of those involved in service provision but gave many examples of finding it seriously wanting. The mothers also said that as they got to know their own children and began to formulate their ideas about disability in general and their own children's needs in particular, they sometimes found that they disagreed profoundly with the attitudes that they found among service providers. They felt, too, that the level, type and quality of available services were often such that it was bound to restrict their children's aspirations and opportunities in unnecessary and unreasonable ways. There was a view strongly held by the majority that some services were rarely made available without a struggle or a fight. Sometimes they had to intervene in situations that were life-threatening for a son or daughter.

It is important to acknowledge, however, that the mothers went out of their way to mention professionals who had delivered a good service. The competent and understanding practitioner or the helpful service was remembered and appreciated in a context where so many crucial things had to be fought for and where standards were not always felt to be high.

Elaine had noticed an improvement in services between the birth of her first and second child. Ann spoke of the psychologist who had been helpful to her son when he was so unhappy that she could not see a way forward. Jean talked very positively of the headteacher of her son's primary school. Margaret said that it was 'wonderful' that Will was now in a school where the staff were so skilled and committed. Mary said that she had been luckier than most people with services. At the beginning, she had had a social worker whom she described as 'brilliant', a very supportive and respectful consultant paediatrician and a very good GP. She felt that this combination had helped to give her an optimistic approach as well as confidence in herself and her son. Victoria spoke with enthusiasm about the orthopaedic consultant who had added to her son's confidence in his adolescence and made him feel that he had achieved a great deal.

When what was offered was not as good as this, the mothers adopted a variety of mediating strategies to improve the situation. Their approach tended to change over time as they gained in knowledge and conviction about key issues. Victoria described the process:

At first, you naturally want to protect your child. Then you get to the stage where you want to start proving your child. Then you want to improve things for them and that's when you have to become a diplomat . . . tread the middle line because if you don't tread the middle line you don't know what the effect is going to be on your child . . . You have to be pushy or your child doesn't get anything but at the same time not get their backs up. It's a very, very fine line . . . and your child's future's on the line.

Ann's view was similar:

> You don't know enough at first. I mean at first you're just sort of gob-smacked and hurting and you don't know enough not to do what you're told. It takes a while for you to have the courage or the knowledge to say, 'Hang on a minute, I don't agree with that', because you assume that they know what they're doing . . . I mean, you have to assume that at first.

Challenging, when necessary, the ideas of the more powerful experts did not come easily. Vera discussed the difficulty of having to overcome her natural shyness in order to ask for things for Matthew's benefit from doctors and other professionals. Deborah said that she had found it quite an ordeal. She pointed out that she was 'only a mother and a very new mother at that'. She found a disparity between her views of her daughter and those of the professionals whom she met in clinics. Deborah felt that her observations of her daughter's progress were not believed. She suspected, too, that the professionals thought that she had not really accepted that Catherine was disabled and saw her as having a rather romantic view of her development. She also found that she differed from the practitioners about what constituted an appropriate upbringing for Catherine and she sometimes found that her attempts to do ordinary things with her daughter met with disapproval. She said:

> They made me feel that everything I did was wrong, as if I could harm her . . . World War Three broke out when I got her a baby bouncer. You see, they said that I was 'encouraging her to go up on her toes' which was thought of as very bad. But I only wanted her to be upright so that she could see around and join in with the rest of us. I felt dreadful then but well, I laugh now.

One reason for the women finding appointments with professionals anxiety-provoking was that at times a great deal could be at stake. They were also aware of the power imbalance that existed in service user–provider relations. They described the ways that they thought through encounters in detail, weighing up what might be the most effective approach. Most started off by being very 'diplomatic', second-guessing what the service providers might be thinking, and moved on to stronger measures only if necessary. When diplomacy failed, a number felt that they had to take a more confrontational stance. Their experiences included challenging decisions through formal procedures and even resorting to calling in the press.

A number also talked about the fact that they found it unacceptable that in order to obtain important services, it was necessary for them to emphasize what were seen as their sons' and daughters' problems and deficits rather than positive achievements and talents. They felt that if they emphasized positive attributes and ways of managing, everyone would be happy to leave them and their children to get on with it.

Margaret described her basic approach to negotiation with professionals in this way:

You have to be very careful that you don't tell them their job . . . they become a little resentful that they can't show what they know . . . their abilities because you're sort of showing yours. You have to be careful how you word things . . . show that you're looking at things from all sides . . . try to take into account all the arguments they're going to use against you . . . You have to be very diplomatic when you make suggestions . . . It's the art of negotiation really. This is what I want, this is what you want and how do we effect a compromise in the middle?

Margaret went on to say that she also thought carefully about the image that she presented in formal meetings, her clothes, her demeanour, as success partly depended on her credibility.

In discussing these issues, the women were painfully aware of the relative weakness of their position, the weight of responsibility that they carried and some of the consequences if they did not get it right. Because significant outcomes often hung on the success or failure of the negotiations, some felt very badly indeed if they did not go well. Fazialt Jan, for example, was frustrated and distressed about her lack of success in obtaining support services for her daughter. Although she had attempted to make contact with the relevant professionals, she was unsure of the structure of services and her lack of English made it almost impossible for her to make headway. Margaret said that she felt guilty if she did not succeed in persuading professionals or their organizations to provide what Will needed. Three of the women talked of the feeling of having to show willing and be particularly helpful when their children were admitted to mainstream school. Unlike the other children attending, theirs were not there quite as of right and so it seemed incumbent upon the women to ensure that no one had an excuse to change their minds.

The mothers spoke of a wide range of things that they had found unacceptable and which they had had to challenge, argue for or work around in some way for the sake of their children. It was not only that helpful services were thin on the ground, it was also that among some professionals, some of the mothers met attitudes about disabled children that they regarded as very disturbing. Similarly, some felt that some services were underpinned by misguided notions of what would meet disabled children's needs most effectively.

Jean and Deborah spoke of early experiences of coming face to face with attitudes among service professionals which they felt signalled some of what would come later, assumptions about disabled children that would need to be challenged throughout their lives. Jean explained that it had never occurred to her not to accept her son but she soon began to realize that not everyone saw things that way:

It started from the day we were walking out of that hospital and a sister, a nursing sister, came over to me and said, 'You realize you don't have to take him home with you, don't you?' and I said, 'I'm sorry, I don't know what you're talking about.' She said, 'Well, you don't have to take him home.' I said, 'No, I'm sorry, he's my son and that's it'. And I think it all started from then. And you sort of put a barrier up then and you think, 'No. This is mine, you know'.

Deborah said that she was grateful to the special care team that saved her daughter's life when she was born but found a different set of attitudes among some others in the hospital. She felt that because Catherine had brain damage, death was seen as being in the natural order of things. The chaplain had come to see her and suggested that if a flower were not perfect, it was better for it to wither and die. She felt that they just wanted her to forget about Catherine: 'They wrote her off. She was the one that didn't work out.' She began to form the opinion that in the eyes of many professionals, disabled children were not as valuable as their non-disabled peers. This view was confirmed by another experience which she regarded as hurtful and dehumanizing. She described how a consultant used her young daughter in a clinical demonstration and compared her with her non-disabled brother:

> And I went into this room and it was a shock to see all these people. I hadn't been prepared you know . . . to walk into such a crowd. All I could see was this sea of white coats . . . They should have prepared me, shouldn't they? . . . In the lecture theatre, when they described my daughter in front of me . . . I thought it was very insensitive. We were an interesting case and Catherine was just a statistic . . . He said, 'Notice how she's doing this and that', and then they'd use long words again . . . picking flies with her, which is hard for a mother to take, and then, came the flippant remark about my son, 'Oh and that one's normal', and then they started comparing them.

Following the diagnosis of Deuchenne muscular dystrophy, Destiny's son had also been the subject of a clinical demonstration. Like Deborah, she had found the experience upsetting and insensitive both to herself and her son.

Jean, too, described a number of experiences that had convinced her that her son was regarded as less important than non-disabled children when it came to medical treatment.The most significant was related to his heart condition, which Jean felt sure had remained untreated because Robert had Down's syndrome. She said that they had been told by the community medical officer that he had a 'slight heart mumur'. He had not been referred to a specialist and it only transpired that he, in fact, had a serious condition when an anaesthetist checked his medical notes on admission to hospital for a tooth extraction. The anaesthetist, Jean said, would not give an anaesthetic but suggested referral to a cardiologist. She said:

> We were told he would have had the treatment . . . if Rob had been a normal child with this heart problem, he would have had the treatment that he was supposed to have. We are convinced of it and there are a lot of other parents in the same boat, though not necessarily with heart conditions . . . but with other conditions, that have got the same feeling as us from doctors . . . 'they're handicapped so it doesn't matter.'

Destiny's son was diagnosed as having Deuchenne muscular dystrophy at the age of nearly 9 years after protracted and difficult contact with the health services. She spoke in detail and with considerable distress about the way that she had struggled for a very long time to persuade people that there was something worrying about his health and development. She described her repeated and persistent efforts to get help for Nik. She believed that the fact that she was a young, lone parent made it easier for professionals not to take her concerns seriously and to write her off as overanxious and lacking in knowledge. She described how, following the diagnosis, she had been given no information and was left to find out about Nik's condition and its consequences from a library. As a result of having not been listened to for so long and of being offered no trusted support, she decided that in future she would cut professionals out of her own and her son's life as much as possible.

Mary was positive about many of the services that she had received but gave two examples of incidents where she had had to intervene strongly to ensure Steve's safety or well-being. On one occasion prior to Steve's having surgery, Mary, unusually for her, made a formal complaint about the approach of a doctor who was not only rude but whose comments made it clear that he had not even read her son's notes. She had also had to press one doctor quite hard to ensure that he investigated whether Steve's shunt was blocked. The doctor was adamant that this was not the problem and became angry when Mary insisted. She was proved right and she said:

> The doctor was quite bolshie about it and I had to stand up to him. Time was going on and it was quite dangerous . . . Because I pushed him, he did something about it. Otherwise, he'd have left him and that doesn't bear thinking about . . . When Steve came back from theatre, the doctor said, 'Oh it was the valve', but he never apologized.

Negotiation and mediation was by no means confined to health service settings. Angela spoke of a very harrowing incident that happened at Louise's school and which had to be tackled. At the age of 12 years Louise had come home one day in a very distressed state. After a long and painful discussion and elimination of possibilities, it transpired that during her swimming lesson, a male assistant had sexually abused her. Because of communication difficulties, she had not been able to tell anyone at school. As well as discussing it with Louise, Angela had reported the incident and made sure that it was dealt with appropriately. Her view of it was this:

> That was one of the worst things that happened. You push it to the back of your mind and close the doors on it because it's something you can't believe happens . . . He thought that because she was handicapped, he could get away with it and that it didn't matter . . . which is really what must have been going through his mind . . . They think that because the person's handicapped, that overrides their feelings, their rights as a person and everything else.

Ann found it offensive that people often seemed to regard disabled children as candidates for charity and that some of this spilled over into service provision. In the current economic climate, children were even sometimes dependent for essential equipment on a local newspaper's Christmas appeal:

> I hate that appeal . . . people who throw money at disabled kids. They have a mega time raising money and then they chuck it at disabled kids . . . It really incenses me . . . it doesn't help disabled kids really . . . but it's the feel-good factor for the people doing it . . . they really feel they've done something . . . usually only for pretty kids and if that child was 30, nobody'd be interested.

A number of the women spoke of their battles over schooling. Jane, Deborah, Ann and Victoria had resisted the assumption that special schools were appropriate for their sons and daughters and had succeeded in gaining places for them in mainstream education. This had been achieved by a combination of persistence, persuasion and use of more formalized procedures. The preferred outcome had not always been easily accomplished. Victoria said that the hardest thing was 'smiling whenever necessary and keeping everybody sweet'. Her son had gone to special school initially and she had been unhappy about the standard of education there compared with that received by her non-disabled daughter. She could not accept that his mobility difficulties should preclude him from having what she regarded as a decent schooling and mixing with local children of his own age. Ann's reasons for negotiating mainstream education were similar:

> I just wanted him to have the same chance as everyone else . . . to make friends locally, to be with friends locally and to go through the same schooling as them.

Other women spoke of the difficulty of obtaining agreement over the further education provision that they felt was appropriate for their sons and daughters. When funding had been refused, Angela felt that the time had come to do battle:

> I think I'm not as pushy as I should be. I find it difficult and I don't know where to draw the line. But there have been times when I've surprised myself, written letters and other things, which I'm not very good at doing normally. But because it's for Louise, I did it. I feel very strongly that she should go to college because the other girls have had that chance. I think it should be her right.

Vera, usually quite shy, described an eleventh hour confrontation to ensure that Matthew could go to a specialist college:

> I was ringing up everywhere to see what the hell was happening. I'd got different numbers, different names and I was having a go at all of them over it. 'What's going to happen to Matthew? What about his future? Where's he going to go?' I was ready to ring up the papers, to have a go . . . to get them to put it on the front headlines . . . Well, I've never done

that before in my life but you've got to fight . . . You see he can't do it himself . . . Well, a woman came to see me on the Friday that he was due to start on the Monday and she says that she's got to talk to some others first. I said, 'Never mind the others. It's Matthew that counts . . . You talk to Matthew', and I walked out and left her with him . . . Well, after that the decision came through.

Community care services had also proved to be a problem for some. Fazialt Jan's daughter was a day student at a specialist college but her mother felt that Shamim's life was too restricted by their circumstances and by the lack of support services made available to them. While she made it clear that she and Shamim had a strong relationship and that she wanted them to continue to live together, she did not feel that it was good for Shamim to be thrown together with her so exclusively. She wanted her daughter to be able to go out independently sometimes and to have friends and her own social activities. She also felt that if there were some aids and adaptations in the house, Shamim would have a greater chance of choosing what she did while she was in the home instead of having to rely upon her mother. Fazialt Jan described in some detail her unsuccessful attempts to tackle these problems and to try to make contact with the relevant services. The need for these services and the difficulty she had experienced in negotiating and accessing them, was the major focus of the discussion with Fazialt Jan. Two of the other mothers also described the lengthy and tiring negotiations that were involved in order to obtain an often quite limited range of aids and adaptations.

Their work as mediators trying to obtain services for their children was ongoing and often time-consuming and stressful. Some of the mothers had difficulty in finding out basic information about their children's entitlements and others discovered quite significant services by chance. Even when they succeeded, things rarely happened easily and there was usually something to be challenged, sorted out or chased up.

The explaining work: face to face with sons and daughters

As is clear from the previous sections of this chapter, the women in the study were offering personal care and attention to their sons and daughters over a protracted period and this meant that they were in the position to witness at close hand many things that they felt simply could not be allowed to pass unremarked. We have already heard their accounts of some of the mediating work that they undertook in an effort to change the minds, behaviour and policies of other people and organizations. In this section, we hear from them about the mediating work that they undertook directly with their disabled sons and daughters: the things that they did to try to influence their outlook and shape their perceptions of the world in ways that were in keeping with their interests. Their children were often directly involved as witnesses or participants in incidents or events which the mothers saw as having a negative impact on them. This made it imperative for the women to react. In addition to reacting to negative incidents and experiences, however, they also felt a responsibility to be proactive in creating circumstances that would foster their sons' and daughters' development and well-being.

When the mothers talked about the face-to-face discussions that they had had with their disabled sons and daughters, they again described strategies and activities characteristic of the approach that they took to the upbringing of children more generally. Mary, for example, put it this way:

> We just brought him up in the normal way really, to mix with people . . . and encouraged him to be outgoing . . . he's very outgoing . . . We did that from the beginning . . . It didn't occur to us to do anything different.

In addition, however, their approach had different features which took into account the dimension of disablement. While their disabled children had many of the same needs as those who were non-disabled, they were having to live with some very different experiences. As we have seen, they frequently encountered assumptions, behaviours and barriers which their mothers saw as not in keeping with their needs. At the same time as challenging those things directly with the individuals or organizations concerned, the mothers also often felt the need to give their children an interpretation or explanation which gave them a greater sense of ease or comfort about themselves and their position. They also tried to help them to develop self-protective strategies and ways of handling situations actively so as to increase their resilience.

In discussing what they did, the women spoke of the general principles that they tried to follow and which underpinned these aspects of upbringing. The principles were manifested incrementally and in different ways as they carried out the day-to-day business of upbringing and childcare. They described a generalized approach that they developed and augmented little by little over time. In addition, they spoke of the way that they tackled specific topics or incidents that struck them as significant.

The majority talked specifically of the importance of being open with children and of talking about issues that had an impact on them. Ann took comfort from the fact that her son 'had not stopped talking since the moment he was born' and seemed to be able to articulate concerns before they became too big a problem. Mary, Margaret, Angela, Jean, Jane, Victoria and Deborah also put great store by explaining and discussing. Fazialt Jan also said that she and her daughter spoke about everything and she did not wish to keep things hidden from her. Elaine was emphatic about the importance of openness and honesty as long as the approach taken was easy-going and relaxed:

> I've never kept anything back. I've told him everything. I don't believe in hiding things. If you keep things from them, they can get the wrong idea . . . they might worry or blame themselves for being disabled . . . As long as you're always there for them, you can be perfectly straight and honest and you don't have to hide things . . . Always answer truthfully. Nothing is too difficult to talk about.

Being open and honest about something that was potentially hurtful was not always easy, however. The process almost invariably required a great deal of thought and the women described the process by which they deliberated and worked out the best approach to take.

For Destiny, some things were just too difficult to talk about. She had also tried to be as open as possible with Nik but said that she could not yet face discussing with him fully how ill he really was and what all the implications were likely to be.

Angela pointed out that Louise's difficulties with speech made any discussion painstaking and slow. If the subject were at all complex, there was often a process of elimination to be gone through in order to work out what Louise wanted to say. Angela needed to do quite a lot of second guessing.

Vera and Matthew were able to talk about some things and not others. Vera wished that her son were more able to voice his feelings. She had tried to encourage him but felt that he did not like this. It was easier, she said, to talk about the action that they were going to take over something such as the battle for further education funding.

Another theme that came out strongly in discussions with almost all of the women was that they regarded it as crucial over time to give their sons and daughters confidence built on what they regarded as a true sense of self-worth. They saw this as the essential backdrop to almost everything else and they gave examples of the things that they said and did to foster a good inner feeling which they hoped would serve their sons and daughters well. This was seen as particularly important in the face of so many circumstances which could conspire to make them feel anything but confident.

Ann said this of her aspirations for John and what she tried to do:

> All I ever wanted was for John to be at peace with what he is and to accept it . . . He seems fairly together and he's always been fairly together. I've never had him come home weeping, saying, 'Why me?' . . . I think he really likes himself and that's all I've ever aimed for. I don't know how that's come about, I really don't . . . I've just been very positive about his achievements and let's face it, he had a very good role model in Dave . . . the way he was with his disability.

Jane talked about Phil's going to a college of further education in a similar way:

> I don't care if he doesn't achieve anything there . . . I mean in the academic sense. And that might sound ridiculous but I just wanted him to be confident, wanted him to feel good about himself. He'd been through so much that he had to get his self-esteem back and that was very, very important.

Elaine emphasized the importance of encouraging her son to be confident enough to take charge of his own life. She felt that the degree of independence that he would be able to achieve would depend largely on his confidence to manage a wide range of situations. This included, where necessary, seeking appropriate assistance for things that he could not manage unaided.

She gave many examples of encouraging Jonathan gradually to gain this confidence in his own ability. She said that she felt very confident in him herself and gave him a clear message that, given time and appropriate support, he would make even more progress and increase his choices in life.

In the context of these strongly-held values, the mothers reported the ways that they talked to their sons and daughters about incidents, processes and ways of the world that they felt were not in their interests or could prove hurtful to them in some way. It is crucial to recognize how painful some of this work was for the mothers, too. One standard approach, which most took at some point, was that of adopting the position of ally to their son or daughter and locating the problem firmly elsewhere, if that was how they saw it. This might simply entail a dismissive remark made in passing or might involve the mothers and their children in a detailed, one-off discussion or an ongoing set of exchanges.

One of the public ordeals that the children and young people consistently faced was that of strangers staring and making insensitive comments when they went out. Jean said that these things were wounding to Rob, as was often evident from the hurt look on his face. Of such times, Jean said:

> There's a phrase we use. I say, 'You've got a big heart, Rob.' I say, 'They're being stupid. You take no notice. You've got a big heart.'

Jane also talked about such incidents and how unsettling they were for Phil:

> If I felt that he was getting upset I've sort of said things like, 'Take no notice Phil. They're the ones with the problem, you know and you just have to rise above it . . . If people stare at you, one day you'll be able to answer back and say, "All right, I do walk a bit different to everybody else and I can't straighten my arm, but I'm all right!" '.

Angela said that Louise asked why people stared at her in town. Her mother told her that everybody was different and that some people stared because they did not understand, did not make the effort or had not got a 'caring side to them'.

Some of the women encouraged their sons and daughters to combine the 'it's their problem' approach with a show of defiance or a challenging remark. Jean said that people were frequently surprised if Rob stood up for himself in the face of other people's prejudice. Some of the women described how they contented themselves with a collusive aside of the 'excuse me I'm a person, too' variety, spoken directly to their sons or daughters in the presence of whoever had been insensitive. Ann said that she hoped and expected that it could go further and that this generation of young people would be able to fight for themselves: 'That was our aim, that's what we wanted.'

Victoria's understanding was that a large proportion of problems could be put down to the way that disabled children and adults were treated as 'second-class citizens', a view that she had shared with her son in different forms over a period of time. She felt that while Paul sometimes wished that she would stop 'banging the drum', he had probably absorbed this perspective from her. She said that she felt that in recent years this had been helpful to him in that he had stopped thinking of the experience of disability only as an individual injustice and had begun to 'take the broader view'. She said that she would not be surprised to see him becoming a campaigner for disabled people's rights. As far as Victoria was concerned, part of being treated as a second-class citizen was Paul's being placed automatically in a special school which she felt provided inferior education to that offered to his sister. At that time in their area, it was regarded as extremely unusual for a child with Paul's impairments to go into mainstream school and there were some uncomfortable times during the two years that it took to bring about his transfer from the special school. Victoria said that she talked to Paul about what they were doing at every stage and why. She had tried to make sense of it by emphasizing to him that they thought that it would be better if he went to the same school as his elder sister, did the same sort of lessons that she did and made friends with the children who lived nearby. She had wanted to offer him this perspective and sense of direction without placing him in a difficult position during his remaining time at the special school.

A number of the mothers spoke about discussions that they had had with their children specifically about the origins of their impairments and also about their feelings about being disabled young people. A number remarked that both their children's feelings about being disabled and the need to discuss it varied from time to time.

Elaine, for example, said that she had always regarded it as important to explain to Jonathan in a matter-of-fact way about his impairments and what had probably caused them. She had tried to demystify things by being very straightforward. He had, however, gone through a patch when he was a little younger, of asking why he was disabled in a way that required a different discussion. Elaine had tried to emphasize to Jonathan about what he was like as a whole person and that his disability was as much part of him as anything else. She said, 'I'd sort of say, "Hey, you! You're you and that's that and we love you! All right?"'

Deborah said that she and Catherine were close and had shared a great deal about other people's reactions to disability:

> She knows about people's attitudes . . . 'Because I can't speak, they think I'm simple' . . . It's her one regret that she can't speak very clearly. She doesn't mind not walking very well but she does wish that she spoke a bit better because people equate that with being thick.

This was one reason why Deborah saw it as particularly important to encourage her daughter to write and publish her poetry. Through her writing, she could express herself with ease and communicate fluently.

External events or a particular life-stage sometimes triggered the need for discussions between the mothers and their sons and daughters. Angela said that Louise usually raised important personal issues when she was helping her into bed at night. If she wanted to talk about being disabled, it was usually a sure sign that something upsetting had happened to her or that there had been a particular incident that had started her thinking about the implications.

For some of the young people, the need or the wish to talk was connected with a disturbing realization that they could not necessarily aspire to the things that their non-disabled peers took for granted. For example, Victoria said that during adolescence Paul had gone through a time of being extremely angry and resentful. He had wanted to talk repeatedly and in detail about how his impairments had come about and became convinced that his parents had let him down by not taking legal action against the health service. He had been overwhelmed for a period with a sense of individual hurt and injustice. Victoria felt that her son was extremely unhappy at this time because he had become unsure about whether he could keep up with his able-bodied mates. It began to hit him quite forcefully that the sort of future social and personal life that they seemed to have in mind might not be so easy for him to achieve. His relationships with his friends altered and he became much more isolated for a while. Breaking into a new social circle when he went to college had not been easy either. Throughout this time, it had been important to keep talking and to 'hold on in there and keep trying to convince him that these things need not necessarily be beyond his grasp'. This had, however, been very difficult and upsetting for everyone. It took a year at college, a long time in a young person's life, before he felt at ease with an accepting group of friends, had a good social life and felt happier again.

Other women, too, spoke of the way that their sons and daughters came face-to-face in adolescence with projected differences between their personal lives and those of their non-disabled peers. Deborah said that until Catherine was about 16, she had always spoken quite confidently about 'when I get married' and 'when I have a house of my own'. Deborah went on to say that it had hit like a thunderbolt when a neighbour's son left home and his mother had spoken in a way that showed that she assumed that, by contrast, Catherine would always live with her parents. Catherine and Deborah had assumed no such thing though they were under no illusions about some of the barriers to be faced. Deborah said that her own and her daughter's discussions had reflected her hope that Catherine would be able to live independently and also have a family of her own:

> I'd like her to marry and have children . . . I don't know whether it will happen . . . I do hope so . . . I do want her to have someone.

Marriage and children had been the subject of important and sometimes upsetting discussions between Angela and Louise, too. When her sister was planning her wedding, it became clear to Louise that things which were part and parcel of the others' expectations were probably going to be much harder for her to come by.

> That upset her . . . it hit her quite hard, I think because I don't think she'd ever thought of it before. She'd just thought about growing up and thought like we all tend to think about growing up and then it hit her

that her limitations to relationships probably would be more than the other girls. When it hit her that she might not be getting married . . . not definitely but probably and that she might not be able to have children, she turned around and asked about babies. She loves children and she said would she have any children . . . ? That was a real shock to actually talk about it. And you have to say it's possible but there's no way on earth that she could look after a baby . . . she'd have to have somebody to do it for her . . . I said nothing's impossible and every situation can be worked on but it might not happen for her . . . Oh but talking about it was very hard because I know how she feels about little ones.

Because Ann was aware that there was likely to be a difference between John's physical development at puberty and that of many of his friends, she felt that she had to take the initiative to talk with her son very explicitly about some aspects of sexual development and experience. Had she not done so, she said, she feared that he would have been in a very difficult position with his peers. The discussions were made all the harder because his father who would normally have expected to deal with these matters, had recently died.

I think the worst time was puberty . . . trying to explain so that he'd know all the right buzz words, so that he'd know what it meant when his mates were talking about all that stuff . . . having to explain everything and then . . . and this was hard . . . saying, 'I don't know but it might not happen to you' . . . That was not easy but I had to do it just so that he didn't feel stupid in front of his friends . . . because there's a lot of covering up goes on.

Another difficult area was to do with ways of making children and young people aware that the world could be a dangerous and hostile place without raising their anxiety excessively and reducing their confidence. While a number of the mothers mentioned their sons' and daughters' vulnerability in this regard, Angela and Jane discussed it at some length. Both had had experiences of trying to help their children when they had been abused or bullied.

Jane talked of trying to get Phil to accept that he was, in the eyes of some, an easy target. She tried to help him to think about safety in numbers and other practical strategies for avoiding the aggression of others. She also described how at 16, her son's behaviour had become very difficult for her to manage and that she had not been able to work out what was happening.

I wasn't coping at all and you know. I'd been trying to get to the bottom of what was wrong with him because his behaviour was atrocious. He'd dig his nails into my arms and really hurt me and hurt himself. I just caught hold of him one day and I said, 'What on earth is the matter with you? You know, you must talk to me!' And he just said that he wished he was dead . . . It was awful and then he told me that he didn't want to go to school again . . . A boy had been bullying him and Phil couldn't retaliate . . . and I think this boy really hurt him, not just physically but mentally.

Besides talking with the school and with her son, Jane had involved a psychologist to talk with Phil. She had not felt that this was a situation that she could deal with alone.

Angela wanted Louise to continue to have more opportunities for independence from her family, including work experience. She felt that it was important to prepare her daughter for the fact that not everyone would be as supportive as those at home and in college without being too negative.

> She has to go out and try things for herself but she's got to be aware that it's not always going to be sweetness and light.

She also talked about the way that she had dealt with the incident of sexual abuse which Louise had experienced at the age of 12 years. She felt that it was important not to leave her daughter in any doubt about the fact that she and other children had a right to be protected from this sort of assault and she was very concerned that Louise's feeling of self-worth should not be damaged. Angela said that now she could not help but feel on her guard and that she had talked to Louise about it:

> You know what's right and wrong and you know if anybody ever did anything to you in any way, shape or form that you knew was wrong, you must always try and let someone know. And don't ever be fobbed off and don't ever give up. If somebody does something that they shouldn't do, you keep on trying until somebody understands you . . . I'm trying to do it without being too frightening . . . I try to make her aware that if it did happen again, she mustn't just sit back and take it.

The majority of the mothers mentioned in some form or another their concerns about their sons' and daughters' futures and their vulnerability. While some had confidence that it was possible for them to live an independent, fulfilling and secure life, others expressed deep-seated anxiety about whether their needs would be met adequately when parents, particularly their mothers, were no longer with them.

Consequences

The women described a variety of consequences of having this close and singular relationship with their disabled sons and daughters. The majority specifically spoke of the ways that they, as individuals, had been changed by the experience.

All of the mothers commented on the consequences of having to challenge service providers or deal with unfamiliar situations in order to get what their sons and daughters needed. Over time, they had undoubtedly become more outward-going and had grown in competence and confidence. There were costs, however, and 10 of the women spoke of the substantial stress and anxiety that this had caused them at various times.

A number pointed out that before having their children, they had held attitudes about disability not dissimilar to those that they now found unacceptable. The majority had been uninformed or had given it little thought. The experience of bringing up a disabled child had changed all that and in addition, according to four of the women, it had had the effect of making them more aware of other groups that they saw as vulnerable or likely to be given a raw deal.

Several talked of feeling that they and their lives had been enriched in unanticipated ways through their relationships with their disabled sons and daughters. The majority pointed out that they had a lot of good times with their children, something that they suspected was not readily appreciated by those who had not had the experience.

Despite this, there were restrictions placed on both mothers and children by a combination of needs and circumstances. Essential care, support and assistance was being given or arranged by the mothers over a protracted period and this undoubtedly limited their choices and room for manoeuvre in some key ways, including working outside the home. At times for some, the work involved, the circumstances in which it was carried out and the accompanying stress meant that it felt virtually impossible to focus on any aspect of their identity other than that of being the mother of a disabled son or daughter.

In addition, more than half of the mothers raised their concerns about how to ensure that a relationship which was of necessity, closer than most between mothers and children did not become overprotective or claustrophobic from the young person's point of view. Eight spoke of very clear aspirations for their sons and daughters to live separate lives from them in the future but they questioned themselves about whether they were currently 'doing too much', 'taking over' or being 'overpowering'. Jean joked at her own expense about the days when her son drew the line by going into his room and putting a 'keep out' notice on the door. Even Destiny, in one of the most taxing and harrowing situations imaginable, was still concerned about whether she was getting the balance right in this respect.

Victoria and Jane described how they felt that during particularly unhappy periods in their sons' lives, they as mothers, had become 'soft targets'. Circumstances meant that they and their sons were in each other's company without the usual escape routes. When the boys had been angry about their position and distressed about external events, Victoria and Jane felt that they had taken it out on the nearest person in the firing line.

One major worry expressed by more than half of the women was that because so much hung on this particular relationship, they could not help but be concerned about what would happen to their sons and daughters if something happened to them. The more isolated and unsupported the woman felt, the greater her worries tended to be in this respect.

While the women talked of worries and potentially negative consequences of being so close, they also spoke creatively of the very positive side of confiding and supportive relationships with their sons and daughters.

Concluding comments

The 12 women all had some experiences in common. They had all played a central role in the lives of their sons and daughters throughout childhood and this was still maintained as they entered adulthood. All of the women had concerns about the way that their sons and daughters were perceived by others and about the barriers that they faced. The services and facilities which would have made it possible for them to live a more fulfilled life had not always been readily available. Sometimes it had been necessary to fight very hard indeed to gain access to things that they regarded as essential for their children's well-being. The majority had a sense, too, that opportunities for disabled children and adults were improving but that there remained a lot of progress still to be made.

There were also variations in their experiences. For example, those whose financial circumstances were more limited had fewer choices and less room for manoeuvre than the other women. Isolation and a lack of personal support was particularly a problem for Fazialt Jan and for those who had been lone mothers for some time. Jean's deteriorating health was distressing in its own right and also because of the effect that she felt it was having on her relationship with her son. Destiny's desperation about her son's fragile condition was marked and took an enormous personal toll. Ann's relationship with her partner, Dave, who was disabled, shaped her views about disability and how to deal with some of the significant matters in her son's life.

Despite the variation in experience, all of the women had taken an active role as mediators with other individuals or organizations and systems. They had interceded and negotiated on their children's behalf to try to bring about change and in turn, had worked directly with them in an effort to make them feel better about themselves or situations that they faced.

It is clear from the women's stories that they felt that circumstances beyond their control dictated much of what they had to take on both at home and elsewhere. Their accounts also demonstrate how despite or sometimes in response to those constraints, they show considerable creativity, skill and dogged determination in seeking solutions to the problems that they and their sons and daughters face.

 **3**

The things that mothers do

The experiences and opinions of the 12 West Midlands women are interesting and important in their own right. When we consider other relevant research and writing, however, there are strong indications that they also have a great deal in common with other mothers of disabled children. There is much in the literature about the population of disabled children and their families in Britain which echoes the 12 mothers' descriptions of their lives, the issues that preoccupy them, the needs to be met and the tasks to be accomplished. This not only includes their work as mediators but also describes situations that make mothers feel that mediation is necessary and justifiable. Apart from the fact that reference to a wider body of research enables the discussion usefully to proceed beyond the confines of one small-scale study, it also goes some way to providing answers for those of the women who asked, 'Is it just me?' and who wished to know whether they were unusual in feeling and doing this or that.

The purpose of this chapter, then, is to contextualize the experiences of the 12 women by introducing major themes on the lives of mothers of disabled children more generally. I shall draw mainly on British empirical research to explore what is documented about the roles they adopt, the tasks they routinely undertake and the problems they face. I shall also look at their perceptions of issues they regard as important, their approaches to solving key problems as well as experiences that they find positive.

In addition to the available body of research, I shall also rely on a further, very valuable source that offers insights into the lives and priorities of those concerned: books and papers written by mothers of disabled children themselves. These have increased in number over the past two decades. Some consist of personal stories, some are handbooks for other parents, while some draw on their own experiences and those of others to advocate for changes in attitudes, policy and practice (for example, Hannam 1975; Boston 1981; Family Focus 1983, 1984; Sheik 1986; Clarke *et al* 1989; Gupta 1989; Mason

1992; Murray 1992). Literature that helps to illuminate some aspects of the mothers' lives by theorizing caring and motherhood will be considered in later chapters.

Mothers, fathers, parents or families

When the existing literature is explored in an effort to discover what is known about the lives of mothers of disabled children, however, one immediate problem presents itself. Although there is existing research that differentiates between the activities and experiences of fathers, mothers and other members of their households, a great deal of American and British literature, as Traustadottir (1991: 212) has observed, has had a tendency to treat the family as the smallest unit of analysis. She points out that gender is frequently ignored as a socially important variable and consequently the difference between mothers' and fathers' experience is sometimes hidden, as is the complex and gendered nature of caregiving.

Similarly, the term 'parent' often masks differentiated roles and on the face of it, leaves us little the wiser about the respective thoughts, feelings and activities of mothers and fathers. However, a closer examination of the samples in some studies of parents' experiences, reveals that in many cases the vast majority of those who participated were, in fact, mothers. When these studies are taken together with those that focus more specifically on men's and women's different parenting roles within households, a clear picture of the lives of mothers of disabled children begins to emerge.

The patterns of informal care provided by mothers and fathers of disabled children reflect patterns of childcare and other forms of informal caregiving in households more generally. Usually in two-parent households the involvement that fathers and mothers have with their disabled children is different in quality and quantity and it is well-documented that it is the mothers who carry the main responsibility for the care and upbringing of their disabled children (Baldwin and Glendinning 1981; Glendinning 1983, 1986; Read 1991; Traustadottir 1991; Abbott and Sapsford 1992; Atkin 1992; Beresford 1994, 1995; Parker and Lawton 1994). A national survey of 1100 households with a disabled child revealed that in 96 per cent of cases, the mother was identified as the person most responsible for providing care (Beresford 1995).

Mothers undertake a greater volume of the work overall and this cannot be fully explained simply by the fact that in two-parent households, fathers are more likely than mothers to undertake paid employment outside the home. Even when fathers are unemployed or at home for other reasons, the caring workload and responsibility is not distributed equally.

Also, when fathers are involved in the caring and upbringing of a disabled child, they and the mothers undertake different types of tasks. The ongoing, day-to-day care, particularly intimate personal care, most often falls to mothers who frequently undertake the physical and practical tasks too. Fathers tend to take on some of those practical and physical jobs which do not include personal care and assistance and also undertake tasks related to the children's leisure activities from time to time or on a regular basis (Atkin 1992).

It is important to recognize that there are large numbers of women who, as lone parents, carry the full responsibility for the care and upbringing of their disabled children anyway. A greater proportion of households with disabled children have lone mothers compared with the general population (Beresford 1995). While some parents report their adult relationships strengthened by the experience of having a disabled child, the evidence from the OPCS surveys is that there is an increased risk of relationship breakdown (OPCS 1989). Mothers of disabled children have both a greater chance of becoming lone parents and a reduced likelihood of repartnering at the same rate as other lone mothers. Older women and those with severely disabled children are more likely to be affected in this respect (Hirst 1991; Baldwin and Carlisle 1994).

There is no suggestion here that all women should seek partners or that lone parenthood is inevitably a more impoverished personal experience for mother or child. These findings are important, however, because of the limitations on household income that often go hand in hand with lone parenthood and because of the fact that the majority of those mothers of disabled children who live with a male partner identify them as the most valuable source of practical and emotional support. While one in five report getting only limited help from a partner, others identify what they regard as quite high levels of back-up (Beresford 1995).

Despite any help that they receive from partners and others, the mothers, nevertheless, remain the main caregiver in the majority of households. Graham's discussion on women's informal health work inside and outside their households is not focused exclusively on mothers who have disabled children but is highly pertinent to them (Graham 1985). She describes how the women take continuous and ultimate responsibility for the maintenance of children's health, their recovery from sickness as well as orchestrating social relations within the home and solving problems when these relationships go awry. Graham argues that not only do mothers cope with the physical demands and restrictions but it is they who also feel an ongoing and primary responsibility for the happiness, health and development of the children. The buck stops with them.

Similarly, Morgan (1996: 105) itemizes what is involved when women care for children with health problems. They provide physical care and monitoring in relation to the children who are ill and manage their fears and frustrations. At the same time, they handle the adjustments required by other family members, some of whom may be resentful. In doing this, he argues, they draw on their own emotional resources and exercise emotional control. The literature on disabled children and their households is replete with examples of mothers concerning themselves with the issues and activities identified by Graham and Morgan (for example Glendinning 1983; Beresford 1995).

In addition, as Graham (1985) has pointed out, the mothers' informal health work means that they also inevitably end up as the go-betweens, the mediators between the household and the formal health and welfare system outside. The key role played by mothers of disabled children in this respect is well-documented (Strong 1979; Sloper and Turner 1982; Glendinning 1983, 1986; Read 1991; Beresford 1995). In two-parent households, fathers of the children may have difficulty in attending appointments (Beresford 1995) and may tend to become involved for non-routine matters (Strong 1979).

Mothers of disabled children, then, are likely to play a distinctive and pivotal role both at home and in the outside world. It is important to recognize the enduring and long-term nature of this role. The tasks to be accomplished may change over time but many mothers will find themselves having a very close and protracted involvement with their sons and daughters. The options for each to live independently of the other are drastically reduced compared with the experience of non-disabled young people and their families (Hirst and Baldwin 1994). In order to understand that relationship, it is necessary to consider in more detail the needs which have to be met and the nature of the work that the women, as main caregivers, undertake at home and elsewhere.

Caring at home

While the upbringing of all children can be taxing, there is no doubt that the care of a severely disabled child frequently makes demands that go a long way beyond what is usually required of parents of non-disabled children (Baldwin and Glendinning 1981; Sloper and Turner 1982; Glendinning 1983; Read 1991; Baldwin and Carlisle 1994; Beresford 1995). The amount of direct caring work with the child tends to be greater, more exacting and more complex than with other children.

Whether at birth or later, if a woman finds herself the mother of a disabled child, there are of course many and varied reasons why she may feel distressed, confused and anxious (Pahl and Quine 1986; Baxter *et al.* 1990; Audit Commission 1994; Hall 1997; Read and Statham 1998). One source of stress is that she may need to learn quickly how to meet her child's quite complex needs for care and assistance and take responsibility for tasks which were hitherto quite outside her experience (Beresford 1995). The evidence is that in this daunting and frightening situation, the majority of mothers simply find a way of getting on with it and embark on a pattern of caregiving that changes them and their lives irrevocably.

Beresford's 1995 national survey confirmed the findings of many other studies on the high levels of personal care and assistance being offered by mothers to their severely disabled sons and daughters of all ages. Help is frequently needed with bathing, washing, eating, toileting, mobility and communication. Special dietary needs have to be met, medication administered, physiotherapy and other programmes undertaken. Some children need to be watched over or need a great deal of attention and stimulation if frustration is to be kept at bay. In addition, social, communication and behavioural problems are identified as significant in the lives of substantial numbers. It has to

be remembered, as other studies have shown, that this work is not confined to the daytime. Many disabled children need attention during the night for a range of reasons and this can result in disrupted nights, not only for the main caregiver but also for other members of the household (Sloper and Turner 1982; Haylock *et al* 1993; Atkinson and Crawforth 1995).

Beresford's 1995 survey also revealed a 'strikingly high proportion' of very young children who were 'technologically dependent'. These are the children with very complex needs who are now surviving in larger numbers as a result of advances in neonatal care. They are dependent for their continuing survival on highly specialized equipment or procedures, which are increasingly managed by their mothers in the home. The Family Fund has reported on the increase in referrals for families with children who need complex technical support. Their social workers have recorded how they have seen mothers follow the necessary procedures 'with a skill second to none' (Williams 1992: 18).

The literature describes graphically the ongoing and long-term nature of the caring commitments. While some children's needs for care and assistance are undoubtedly reduced as they mature, for large numbers this is not the case. For example, in Beresford's research (1995), four out of five of the young people in the 12 to 14 age group still needed help with self-care. One in two needed a great deal of assistance with washing, dressing, toileting and moving about. Two-thirds needed to be supervised and kept occupied. The point has frequently been made that as a child gains in height and weight, the physical demands on many mothers also become greater.

In addition, Beresford's 1995 survey showed that behavioural, social and communication problems increased in prevalence and severity as children grew older, as did the negative impact that they were seen to have on a range of necessary or desirable daily tasks and activities. Challenging behaviour in an older and bigger child is clearly more difficult to accommodate and manage than in one who is younger and smaller.

As disabled children grow older, their personal, educational and social needs of course also change. If these needs are to be met appropriately, they, like their non-disabled peers, require changing arrangements, responses and services. Sadly, it often seems that within their own homes and elsewhere, the opportunities that would allow them increasing autonomy and the chance for a greater independence from their parents are rather difficult to come by (Flynn and Hirst 1992; Hirst and Baldwin 1994). Whatever the young people and their mothers would otherwise choose, a combination of circumstances often conspire to maintain their close, interdependent relationship over a protracted period. Frequently, mothers can see no other options that are acceptable to them.

Hubert (1993: 112), for example, explains why parents in her study resisted pressure from professionals to allow their adult sons and daughters who had profound learning disabilities to live away from home:

Professionals tell them that it is normal for teenagers to leave home, to become independent of their parents, and abnormal for a mother to devote her life to her adult child. But these parents know their children will never have any real independence and will remain totally dependent on other people for most of their basic needs. In fact, if they left home, they would move into an environment in which they would be even less autonomous than they are now, since their needs and wishes would be less understood by those around them, and in most cases there would be no one prepared to try to interpret the often minute signs that parents have learnt to understand. Thus many would probably live the rest of their lives without ever having another close and reciprocally satisfying relationship.

It is crucial to recognize that the social and material circumstances in the home in which women undertake this taxing level of activity often compound the difficulties that they and their children face.

A great deal of this skilled and demanding work goes on routinely, unsung and in private. Many mothers experience social isolation (Baldwin and Glendinning 1981; Read 1991; Murray 1992; Haylock *et al.* 1993) and find that the informal supports on which other women rely to offset the rigours of childrearing (for example, going to the flats and houses of other women in the neighbourhood and reciprocal childcare and babysitting arrangements) may not be readily available to the mother of a severely disabled child (Meltzer *et al.* 1989; Read 1991; Russell 1991). Women from minority ethnic populations have been identified as particularly vulnerable to some of the most extreme forms of isolation (Baxter *et al.* 1990). While self-help and support groups for families of disabled children may be experienced as helpful by some women, the majority do not join such organizations. Those from minority ethnic groups and those on low incomes are least likely to be members. In addition, these self-help groups do not generally provide childcare and other practical supports (Beresford 1995).

Mothers of disabled children are not unlikely to find themselves living on a restricted budget and may, therefore, not have the choice of buying in childcare or other practical sources of help and diversion for themselves and their child. There has long been overwhelming evidence that bringing up a disabled child has a significant financial impact on the household (Baldwin 1985). Growing up with disability involves substantial additional expenditure. Simultaneously, however, the demands of caring reduce the options that parents, particularly mothers, have for gaining income by entering paid employment outside the home. This combination of factors leaves households with disabled children worse off financially than those in the general population and this can have a substantial negative effect on standards of living and choices available to those involved. Lone parents have been found to be in a particularly vulnerable financial position. There is also evidence that the more severe the child's impairment, the greater will be both expenditure and restrictions on earnings (Baldwin and Carlisle 1994). The chances for women who have disabled children to participate in the labour market and to have a career are drastically reduced and their position in this respect has worsened over the past 20 years (Baldwin and Glendinning 1983; Baldwin 1985; Smith and Robus 1989; Baldwin and Carlisle 1994; Beresford 1995).

It is also crucial to acknowledge that mothers are not unlikely to be providing care for their disabled children in housing conditions that are restricting and unsuitable for child and carer alike (Sloper and Turner 1993; Beresford 1995). Restricted financial resources limit families' choices and leave some in housing of a very poor quality. Families from minority ethnic groups and those on very low incomes have been found to have more severe housing problems than other households. The Family Fund has reported increasing numbers of referrals from families living in what they regard as worsening conditions. Williams (1992) gives the example of Family Fund social workers' experience of visiting disabled children and their families in bed and breakfast hotels where conditions are extremely squalid and hazardous to health and safety.

However, even when families have accommodation of a reasonable standard if judged by general criteria, it frequently does not have the space, layout and adaptations to meet the needs of the disabled child, the main carer and other members of the household. Significant proportions of families move house because their accommodation is unsuitable (Beresford 1995).

Morgan (1996) has emphasized the emotional component of mothers' work in relation to children who have health problems. The growing disabled child who is trying to make sense of some of the frustrating, bewildering and wounding experiences in their lives, is likely to turn to the nearest adult for an explanation. The mother, who is involved in an intimate caring relationship with her child, may be the obvious candidate. She may be the immediately available source of information and opinion (Read 1991). Even when the child does not initiate such interaction, the mother may nevertheless feel that it is her responsibility and wish to find a way of helping her child to make sense of a situation and to feel better. In an open studies project referred to elsewhere (Read 1991), parents of disabled children could identify issues on which they wanted to work together. It is telling that a consistently popular workshop topic was one which dealt with ways of talking with their disabled children about difficult and hurtful matters.

The taxing problems of daily living and caring for the disabled child may frequently be accompanied by understandable anxiety about meeting other competing needs within the household. A picture emerges that is consistent with the model proposed by Graham (1985) and Morgan (1996) whereby women take responsibility for balancing the needs of different family members in order to secure their health and well-being. Studies have consistently reported parents' particular concerns that their other children miss out in a number of ways because of the exceptional demands placed on the household (Glendinning 1983; Meltzer *et al.* 1989). More recent work undertaken directly with the siblings of disabled children supports this view without denying the positive aspects of their experience (Atkinson and Crawforth 1995). Research also reveals the efforts made by parents to even things out, to avoid neglecting their non-disabled children's needs and to limit the restrictions placed on them (Glendinning 1983).

Going out in public

Escape from the confines of home is not always easy for mothers, their disabled children and others in the household. Undertaking activities that others take for granted frequently requires extraordinary energy, planning and organization. Transport problems, a restricted budget and an inaccessible built environment are often cited as barriers to getting out and about. Parents' fatigue, problems with equipment that a child needs to have with them and difficulties with a child's mobility or behaviour are also given as reasons (Beresford 1995). When all these things are taken into account, having a day-trip out, going to the supermarket, getting a haircut or buying a new jumper may not be easily accomplished.

It is not only that this confinement is difficult in itself. As Williams (1993) argues, the experience of these women and disabled children and adults has to be set against general trends in leisure and consumption. Increasingly for many in the population, spending money in out-of-town, large scale facilities is a routine leisure activity. Because of restricted disposable income, distance and transport difficulties, these mothers and their children, particularly those in poverty, are consistently excluded from participating in activities which are increasingly part and parcel of the expectations of others.

Given all of this, the *cri de coeur* from one respondent in a national survey should come as no surprise:

> I would like someone just to give me a pat on the back occasionally and say how well I am doing, just to give me a boost.
>
> (Beresford 1995: 26)

Sadly, however, it is not merely that some women feel the lack of recognition for what they achieve; they have to face something much more unpleasant. A substantial number of mothers in Beresford's 1995 study reported that their concerns about the reactions of members of the public to their children's appearance or behaviour caused them to limit their trips outside the home.

Dealing with other people's negative, thoughtless or ill-informed reactions to their disabled children can be a distressing feature of the lives of many mothers. Parents have described how they feel isolated because their children are perceived by other people to be disturbing and less valuable than non-disabled children (Baldwin and Glendinning 1981; Goodison 1981; Read 1985, 1991). Glendinning (1983: 225) summarizes the experience of those in her study:

> The reactions of members of the public in the street and other public places, and reports in the press and on radio and TV all communicate to parents the dominant responses of society to severe disablement in children. In different ways these messages seemed to lead to the development and reinforcement of a sense of isolation: an awareness of the many ways in which their particular experience of parenthood diverged from the patterns of those around them.

It is not only that mothers experience the hurtful incidents directly them-selves and have to decide what to do there and then, it is also that they may witness the effect on their children. It can be unbearably painful to see their children on the receiving end of insensitive or discriminatory attitudes. It is not only the dramatic and easily recalled incidents that give rise for concern, it is also the eroding process by which the growing disabled child becomes aware incrementally of the inferior social status accorded to disabled people (Read 1991). In recognition of the problems faced by parents and children when they go out in public, one Australian voluntary organization published a guide that was exclusively concerned with how to manage community and public insensitivities (Cronin and Fullwood 1986).

Negative or insensitive reactions are not always confined to encounters with strangers. Studies tend to report mixed responses on the part of neigh-bours, with parents being very appreciative of positive or friendly attitudes (Glendinning 1983). Difficulties with neighbours in relation to the disabled child, however, have been given as the main reason why some families decide to move house (Beresford 1995). Similarly, as Beresford (1995) also reports, support from extended families can be enormously important but an un-favourable reaction to the child from family members can be very distressing indeed. It is not difficult to see why this would be regarded as the unkindest cut.

It is not only adult carers who cope with unkindness, insensitivity or indif-ference. A study on the experience of 29 siblings of disabled children reported that almost three-quarters of them faced bullying or teasing at school because of their brother's or sister's disability. They also reported awkward responses by friends (Atkinson and Crawforth 1995).

Mothers' perceptions of their children

While being a witness to other people's negative reactions to your child can be hurtful and isolating in its own right, there is a further important dimen-sion to be considered. It can be argued that there is likely to be a gap between the mother's view of her child and the views of those outside the immediate household. Other people's perceptions may often be governed by dominant and not very appreciative notions of disability and they may define the child primarily in those terms. For the mother who knows the child intimately, this simply does not square with her experience.

Beresford (1994: 59) points out, 'Parents do not view their child as a dis-ability. They describe their child as an individual who has limitations and diffi-culties arising from the disabling condition'. Mothers are frequently at pains to point out the distinction between the direct caring work that they under-take with their child and other demanding work, such as dealing with service providers, that goes along with having a disabled child in current circum-stances (Read 1985). Whatever the view of others, mothers tend not to char-acterize their disabled children as burdens to be shouldered (Read 1991).

Studies consistently report mothers describing their disabled children with love, pride and appreciation (Glendinning 1983; Goodey 1991; Beresford 1994). They stress the child's individuality, personality and achievements as well as the rewarding and enriching contribution that they make to the two-way parent–child relationship. While it may well be true that research as a whole has had a tendency to conceive of disabled children as passive victims (Priestley 1998), the same cannot always be said of some subjects of research, the disabled children's mothers. In the literature, there are many examples of mothers consistently emphasizing the way that their disabled children act on the world, as opposed merely to being acted upon. This positive view of the child as an active and contributing individual has been recognized as a significant factor which influences how parents cope with demanding situations (Beresford 1994).

Writing by mothers of disabled children themselves reinforces these findings. They are often at pains to dispel assumptions that they have learned to expect on the part of others, by pointing out what their children are *not* as well as what they are:

> But do not think that Emma was a burden. She was not – and is not. A disabled child can be a blessing in a family. Emma certainly is – a loving, tender, vivacious and friendly girl who happens to have fits. She is the most open person I know: thinking about her brings tears to my eyes and whenever I set off in the car towards London to bring her home for the holidays I feel a tug of joy in the pit of my stomach.
>
> (Smith 1989: 169)

Mothers write about how they themselves, and their perceptions are changed through getting to know their child (Murray 1992). Implicitly or explicitly some begin to stress the importance of accepting and valuing greater human diversity, a notion that is reflected in the title of the book, *To a Different Drumbeat*, written by a group of women who have disabled children (Clarke *et al.* 1989). The notion of a different drumbeat seems to challenge the automatic privileging of dominant values and validates the different.

In different ways, mothers may become aware of the tensions that this creates between their own views and those commonly held by others. Beardshaw (1989: 297) wrote, 'learning to treasure my daughter's uniqueness in a world obsessed with "normality" was – and still is sometimes – a very painful thing'. MacHeath (1992: 90) described fundamental changes in her thinking since having her daughter:

> To ignore the issue of disability seems to me now to be ignoring the most fundamental questions of what life is all about. To me, it can be liberating to have Maresa there, reminding me all the time that the most important things in life are not about achieving more and more, or acquiring more and more. The difficulties are those of a society that doesn't know how to listen, laugh, have fun and provide the basic necessities for everyone. When I'm angry, that is what I'm angry about. Maresa

can have as much fun as anybody, but is more often excluded because people haven't the time to listen and play, or because places or things, such as swings in the playground, are inaccessible to her.

In their introduction to the collection of stories written by parents of disabled children, Murray and Penman (1996) highlight the discrimination that they see their children experience daily. They describe how much they have learned from their own disabled children and present themselves as their allies in a struggle to gain things that others take for granted.

It is easy to fall into the trap of thinking of all mothers of disabled children as being non-disabled themselves. Until the 1990s, little attention has been given to the experience of disabled mothers generally (Mason 1992; Thomas 1997) and there are still fewer published accounts of the experience of disabled women bringing up disabled children.

Mason, a disabled woman, has not only recorded her reflections on her own upbringing as a child and her parents' reactions to having her but has also described the experience of having her own disabled daughter. In her accounts of her childhood (Sutherland 1981; Mason 1992) she argues that while her parents' ideas about disability changed as a result of having her, they were nevertheless somewhat hidebound by their lack of experience of disability and the assumptions that went with that. On discovering that they had a disabled child, they were said to be disappointed, frightened and bewildered. Mason, for whom disablement was familiar territory, reacts to the birth of her daughter in a very different way. Motherhood may be frightening and challenging but the fact of her daughter being disabled is not described in the same terms. By contrast, her mood is jubilant and celebratory:

> When I took this little tiny person home, who was lying on a special mattress, all tucked up and asleep at only ten days old, I still felt a sense of euphoria. I remember seeing her on her little bed, on top of my bigger bed, and thinking that she was an angel who had plopped down from heaven as a present for me. A reward for not giving up on life.
>
> (Mason 1992: 116)

Involvement with service providers

Discrepancies of view over a child may also be one of the issues which make for difficulties in another commonplace situation where mothers find themselves side by side with their disabled sons and daughters. In this, I refer to their dealings with service providers, a matter which warrants detailed exploration.

In addition to the direct caring work, having a disabled child necessitates involvement with a multiplicity of different agencies and professionals (Sloper and Turner 1982; Glendinning 1986; Yerbury 1997). This in itself constitutes tiring, time-consuming and often frustrating work. As we have already established, it is taken on primarily by mothers.

Families identify the presence of appropriate and supportive services as a factor that makes a very big difference to their own and their children's lives and often single out for mention a particular professional whom they remember for getting things right (Haylock *et al.* 1993). A good service that meets needs can be a powerful mediator of stress (Sloper and Turner 1982). A supportive working relationship can be developed when a service, such as a school, is perceived by parents genuinely to value and accept their children (Ballard *et al.* 1997). Unfortunately, many do not have this positive experience and it has been consistently reported that for very many parents, dealing with service providers is identified as *the most stressful* part of bringing up a disabled child (Beresford 1995). In other words, contact with those ostensibly there to help and support, can make mothers feel worse.

Across almost two decades, a wide range of literature and official reports record considerable levels of unmet need for quite basic services. There is also substantial dissatisfaction with many aspects of the services that exist, the ways they are delivered and the contact between families and providers.

Beresford (1995: 24) identifies three basic sets of enduring and overarching difficulties between parents and service providers:

- a discrepancy of opinions between parent and professional about the parent's and child's needs, and an unwillingness on the part of professionals to acknowledge parents as experts in the care of their child;
- a confused relationship between parent and professional. Professionals can view parents as a resource for statutory services, as co-workers and clients in their own right. Because of this, professionals find it hard to develop appropriate ways of working with parents;
- lack of coordination between services – a problem compounded by the fact that numerous professionals tend to be involved with these families.

These three areas of potential conflict are intimately related. For example, when a discrepancy of view arises between a service user and a professional, the roles, status and expertise accorded to each, and their respective power to affect the outcome, become very significant indeed.

It is important to acknowledge that conflicts of view between provider and user about children's and parents' needs constitute a long-standing and fundamental problem. For example in 1970, Younghusband *et al.* reported on the concern expressed by mothers about the negative attitudes and lack of understanding on the part of some service professionals. More recent work has also revealed often quite substantial differences of view between many parents and professionals about ways of perceiving disabled children as well as about what are regarded as appropriate lifestyles, aspirations and services (Thomas 1982; Read 1985, 1991; Goodey 1991; Gregory 1991; Haylock *et al.* 1993; Twigg and Atkin 1993; Beresford 1994). Some of these differences of view may be related to issues that impact upon the children's present and future well-being in major ways. For example, disagreements and conflicts of interest over appropriate education are commonly reported (Rogers 1986a, 1986b; Audit Commission 1992; Haylock *et al.* 1993; Beresford 1994). There has also been media coverage about disquiet among parents whose children live with Down's syndrome, that some who have heart conditions may have been precluded from having life-saving or life-enhancing treatment available to their non-disabled peers (BBC 1998).

When disputes or conflicts of opinion arise in encounters between a professional and a mother of a disabled child, the issue is unlikely to be regarded as a straight difference of opinion between equals. The encounters generally take place within a framework and on territory more familiar to and frequently controlled by the professional. Twenty years ago, Strong (1979: 128) explored key features of the interactions between staff and parents (mostly mothers) in his study of paediatric consultations:

> Here parents were both excluded and controlled. They might be partners but they were not equals and the balance of power within the bureaucratic format was one of its most striking features. Although parents had some rights to question and to criticize they could only use these within an overall context of medical dominance. The technical authority given to the doctors was matched by an equivalent authority to control almost every aspect of the consultation's shape, sequence and timing.

Strong (1979) also observes that while the women might be assumed by staff to be loving and competent in their role as mothers, it was also almost universally taken for granted that they were ignorant of those things deemed to be in the area of competence of the professional. Correspondingly, whatever the reality of the competence of the staff, they both assumed and were granted the mantle of expert. He adds:

> Further, even though parents might normally be considered to have the most extensive knowledge of their child and to be the best interpreter of their words, actions and feelings, such knowledge was treated as partial and as able to be overridden when staff saw fit.
>
> (Strong 1979: 132)

When the mother of a disabled child has a genuine difference of view from a member of staff in such circumstances, she may well appreciate the unwritten rules of the game identified by Strong. She may find it difficult to know how to proceed and ensure that her voice is heard without making things worse for herself or her child. Almost 20 years ago, Gliedman and Roth (1980: 150) also observed how the structure of the parent–professional relationship almost automatically transformed the parent into a kind of patient; they summarized the ensuing dilemma:

> As for the parent, the circle is closed and he finds himself in a double bind: either submit to professional dominance (and be operationally defined as a patient) or stand up for one's rights and risk being labelled as maladjusted (and therefore patient-like).

The language may have changed and services may have a more consumerist orientation but it is not unlikely that mothers of disabled children in the 1990s will still be familiar with the basic problems identified by Strong and Gliedman and Roth two decades ago. When there is a dispute between mother and professional, one way of resolving it (for the professional) is to raise questions related to the mother's competence. As Strong (1979: 153) argued:

> Despite the surface neutrality of the ceremonial order, medical work in all these consultations necessarily involved routine and systematic moral investigation. On the one hand, doctors treated parents with the greatest delicacy, on the other hand, they covertly scrutinised their competence and character in a myriad of ways.

Apart from the fact that from their point of view, this impedes progress towards obtaining what they think their child needs, mothers may often find such encounters and the implied criticism of their intentions and actions both wearing and hurtful (Murray 1992).

As Thomas (1982) has observed, there is also a differential emotional investment on the part of parent and professional in the process. In most cases, the whole business simply *matters* more to the mother and to her it can seem very unjust that someone who may not know her child very well and whose involvement is fairly transitory, may have so much of a say (Read 1985).

Strong has also argued that clear conflicts of interest can emerge when professionals and their organizations have aims in addition to those of providing direct care or treatment to the child and the parent. He suggests that in some settings, an emphasis on teaching medical students led to breaches of privacy and confidentiality and reduced the patients waiting in their cubicles to the status of 'auxiliaries in a floating classroom' (Strong 1979: 167).

The women may also be painfully aware that the professionals are gatekeepers to resources that they and their children need in one form or another. The professionals may have the power to operationalize policy at a face-to-face level, their assessments and informal opinions may influence the allocation of scarce resources, their definitions of problems and needs as well as people carry weight and they can impart or withhold information in ways that make a difference to children and their parents.

This is not to suggest a concerted effort or some form of conscious intent on the part of all professionals to treat mothers of disabled children badly and exploit any advantage that they may have over them. Nor can it be assumed that professionals have unfettered power, for many undoubtedly feel that in practice they have very little room for manoeuvre. Nevertheless, it has to be recognized that when they are face to face with the mother of a disabled child, the playing field can hardly be said to be level. When such power relations exist and are assumed to be the natural order of things, there is the ever-present danger that parents' skills, expertise and concerns may be neglected or that they may be seen primarily as assisting the professionals in whatever course of action they deem most appropriate (Cunningham 1983). This state of affairs certainly calls into question any notion of partnership (promoted by the Warnock Report in 1978 and further reinforced by the Children Act 1989) that does not recognize and address the vexed question of the imbalance of power in the relationship (Read 1985; Appleton and Minchom 1991; Stallard and Lenton 1992).

Apart from the issues related to the relationship between mothers and professionals, there is the added problem that services are delivered through complex organizational arrangements that have undergone major changes in the late 1980s and early 1990s (McCarthy 1989; Holliday 1992; Cochrane 1993; Billis and Harris 1996). Evidently it is not only the potential user who finds the system confusing and impermeable, for the Audit Commission (1994) also found it difficult in some agencies to identify who was managerially responsible for childhood disability provision.

Services are also supplied by an increasing range of specialists and it has proved difficult to find a suitable organizational framework through which they can be delivered effectively. The recognition that the diversity of need that exists cannot be satisfactorily met by uniform services has led to calls for more individualized, flexible approaches to planning and provision (Appleton *et al.* 1997; Hall 1997). Children and their parents may have a great deal of contact with substantial numbers of professionals at any one time but the frequency of contact and amount of activity generated does not guarantee a positive outcome or needs being met (Sloper and Turner 1982). On the contrary, McConachie (1997: 5) reports on those parents who

> endure serial assessments of their child, without ever having a discussion with professionals of what they want to achieve for their family, their strengths as parents, their needs and ways of coping, and their priority services for their child.

Provision varies in quality and availability from area to area. There are enormous problems associated with coordination and joint planning between key agencies and disciplines at all levels and an ever-present danger that disabled children and their parents fall through the gaps or become marginalized (Sloper and Turner 1982; Glendinning 1983, 1986; Baxter *et al.* 1990; Gough *et al.* 1993; Haylock *et al.* 1993; Wishart *et al.* 1993; Audit Commission 1994; Social Services Inspectorate 1994; Beresford 1995; Butt and Mirza 1996; Appleton *et al.* 1997; Hall 1997; McConachie 1997; Yerbury 1997). Frequently, parents simply do not know of and are not supplied with information about basic services which might help their child or to which they could be entitled (Sloper and Turner 1982; Stallard and Lenton 1992; Haylock *et al.* 1993).

These are ongoing problems in the lives of disabled children and their mothers but there is evidence that at particular critical points they are likely to be felt most acutely. Key transitional times such as the identification of disablement, entry into the education system and change from children's to adult services have the potential to be particularly hazardous and stressful for children and those close to them (Sloper and Turner 1982; Audit Commission 1994; Baldwin and Carlisle 1994; Hirst and Baldwin 1994; Appleton *et al.*

1997; Read and Statham 1998). At these crucial points, parents and children find themselves facing and making sense of a new and anxiety-provoking situation which can have enormous personal significance and impact. In order to achieve a successful outcome, they have to seek out, absorb and apply fresh, often complex information. Entirely new problems present themselves and new routines have to be found for solving them. Because of the importance of the outcome, the stakes feel very high, the workload increases and so may stress levels.

There can be few mothers of severely disabled children who have an easy or trouble-free life and it has been argued that in addition to everything else, their status as women means that they have to overcome particular barriers in their dealings with service providers (Darling 1979; Read 1985, 1991). One mother described the experience this way:

> We are ordinary people coping with extra pressures, extra illness, extra work . . . Sometimes you need a secretary just to keep track of the appointments. But we don't have secretaries, we have to do it all ourselves . . . If you get upset, they think 'Ah! She's a neurotic woman.' So you have to be careful not to show it.
>
> (Read 1985: 71)

All parents, in particular mothers, have to take the initiative and be very active indeed if they are to access the services and information that is needed (Sloper and Turner 1982). Services are sometimes described as being allocated on a rational basis by service providers. It is more accurate, however, to see them as being negotiated (Twigg and Atkin 1994). Sometimes, depending on the point of view, 'fought for' might be a more appropriate way of describing the process. Fighting for services is not only energy and time-consuming, however, it can also very easily lay mothers open to charges of unreasonable behaviour.

There are some women, however, who experience particular difficulties in finding ways of ensuring that their own and their children's needs for services are met. Sloper and Turner (1982) draw attention to the fact that those families under the greatest pressure because of a combination of stressful life events and very limited resources are least likely to be able to take on the formidable task of persistently and actively seeking what is needed. A number of other studies have highlighted children and families from Black and minority ethnic communities, lone parents and those on low incomes as being vulnerable to having unmet needs for services and support (Baxter *et al.* 1990; Beresford 1994; Shah 1992, 1997). The underrepresentation of poorer children and their families and those from Black and minority communities among users of some provision (for example, family-based, short-term break schemes) has been a cause for concern (Robinson 1998).

It has been argued that culturally responsive and appropriate services are often simply unavailable to Black families. Simply gaining access to essential information verbally or in writing may be exceptionally difficult for those whose mother tongue is not English (Begum 1992; Shah 1997). Attention has also been drawn to the ways in which predominantly white service professionals may misunderstand the needs of disabled children and their parents from minority ethnic communities and stereotype their lifestyles in ways that are damaging to their interests (Sheik 1986; Baxter *et al*. 1990; Gunarantam 1993; Shah 1992). It has also been argued that service providers are sometimes ill-informed about some disabling conditions which mainly affect children from Black and minority ethnic populations and that services for them can be marginal, underfunded and insensitive in their responses (Dyson 1992, 1998).

How mothers manage

When all of this is taken together, it is hardly surprising that there can be an impact on the physical and psychological health of those bearing the brunt. Mothers of disabled children have been found to experience higher levels of stress than others in the general population and, again, lone mothers are particularly at risk. Most families keep going but as Beresford (1994) has observed, the equilibrium that they manage to create is often fragile and can be upset by an unforeseen crisis.

It has also been argued that factors that generate stress or promote personal well-being are complex, suggesting the need to be cautious about generalization (Russell 1991; Baldwin and Carlisle 1994). It would also be a mistake if it were implied that all stress that families experience is related to the fact of having a disabled child in the household (Beresford 1994).

Some work in the 1990s has taken a new approach to the issue of stress and coping in families with disabled children of 12 years and under (Beresford 1994). In a sample of 20 families, the study identified those primarily responsible for the care of the child as being the mothers in all but one of the households. The active strategies that they employed to manage difficulties were then explored. Beresford reported on their considerable creativity and on the enormous range of tactics that they employed. What is interesting about this piece of work is that it consciously construed the mothers as potentially 'active agents' rather than 'passive recipients' in relation to the very substantial problems that they encountered. While the study ackowledged what the women were up against, it resisted a crudely deterministic view of human experience. The approach also gave rise to the suggestion that services which enhanced and strengthened those preferred and characteristic coping mechanisms were more likely to work.

Concluding comments

The considerable body of literature now available offers substantial information, then, about the complexity of the situations in which mothers of disabled children find themselves and the taxing nature of the problems that they face. More than ever before, we also have insights into the women's perspectives on the positive aspects of their lives, the important issues as they define them and the active strategies that they develop to manage and resolve a range of problems and dilemmas.

It is clear that many of the responsibilities and experiences described by the West Midlands mothers are not untypical of those faced by populations of mothers of disabled children more generally. There are similarities in the day-to-day work that they undertake and the things that they need to manage or orchestrate in some way. The sense is strong of women feeling that they are their children's allies and that it falls to them to negotiate or mediate with individuals or institutions on their behalf.

Earlier in the book, I suggested that it is difficult to imagine remaining unimpressed when face to face with women whose lives demand so much of them and who frequently rise to the occasion with such varied and active responses. In many respects, the literature can have a similar impact on the reader. As we have already seen, however, it has not always been the case that women with disabled children have been viewed in such an appreciative way. This is in part at least, to do with misunderstandings or untested assumptions about the nature of disability and the attributes and lifestyles of disabled children and those close to them (Philp and Duckworth 1982; Thomas 1982). It may also be related to assumptions about the nature of motherhood and mothering. The next chapter will focus on ways in which the state of motherhood and the activities of mothering have been theorized and what the consequences are for mothers themselves of a range of influential perspectives being applied to their lives.

 **4**

Theorizing motherhood,
mothering and caring

Introduction

In their accounts of their lives, the 12 West Midlands women explained how they did much of what they did because they were women and mothers. Those who had other children frequently drew comparisons between the approach that they took with their disabled children and that with other sons and daughters. Whether or not there were other children in the family, a sentiment such as 'it's the same with any child', often featured in their explanations. Although they saw differences between the upbringing of disabled and non-disabled children, there were many examples where they felt that it was desirable and sensible to put similar principles and expectations into operation. Likewise, the review of literature on mothers of disabled children revealed that in many respects, the roles that they adopt and the activities that they undertake reflect patterns of childrearing, childcare and, therefore, mothering more generally.

This makes it interesting to give some thought to how we make sense of motherhood and mothering, particularly those aspects relevant to the experiences described by the 12 West Midlands women. By motherhood, we usually mean the social or legal status and by mothering, we refer to the caring or nurturing activities that are often, though not inevitably, associated with it. The ways that both the status and the activities are characterized have considerable implications for those women who are mothers. Theoretical understandings now and in the recent past on motherhood and mothering in general, can help to illuminate some of the particular experiences of mothers of disabled children. In many respects we find that the various ways of viewing mothers of disabled children, which we have noted earlier, reflect contemporary accounts of motherhood more generally. In turn, of course, ways of seeing mothers reflect strongly held notions about women and their place in the world.

There is also considerable overlap between some work on mothering and some on informal caring more generally, mainly because of the centrality accorded to gender. Mothering may have some distinctive features but it can also be seen as just one of the types of informal care undertaken by women. It therefore makes sense to explore both together. Inevitably, because of the nature of what is bound up in the subject, this chapter relies heavily on feminist literature.

Images of mothers: points of view

This book started by trying to understand the perspectives of 12 mothers of disabled children about some important dimensions of their lives. Later on it also relied heavily on research and other literature that drew on mothers' own accounts of what they did and why they did it. I noted that 'letting the people speak', understanding their perspectives and according importance to them had not always been regarded as a valuable enterprise. In that respect, mothers of disabled children had much in common with mothers more generally.

Kaplan (1992: 3) has argued that until the mid-1980s the mother as a subject in her own right had been largely ignored by scholars:

> It was not then so much that the mother had not received attention as that she had been studied from the Other's point of view; or represented as an (unquestioned) patriarchally constructed social function. Few scholars had been interested in her positioning or her social role from *inside* the mother's discourse in whatever context, of whatever type.

Phoenix and Woollett (1991a: 2) come to some similar conclusions. Reviewing the literature on empirical developmental psychology concerned with mothers' interactions with infants and attitudes to childrearing, they conclude:

> Firstly we were struck by the contrast between the attention given to children in developmental psychology and the lack of attention given to their mothers. For while 'normal' mothers have been well researched in developmental psychology, they are generally only discussed as people who are the most important influences on their children. Women's experiences of motherhood and feelings about being mothers are rarely explored but can sometimes be found tucked away in studies about children.

With some exceptions, then, until the 1980s it had apparently not been regarded as legitimate or interesting by most scholars to conceive of the mother as the subject, centre stage. While she made a lot of appearances, she was frequently on the margins, not the main business, not the real topic under discussion. She was spoken about rather than speaking in discourses that centred principally on other things and other people.

When the mother came into focus, she was not always well-served by the attention. She was sometimes idealized for her service to her family, her nurturing of children, but she was also often the brunt of attack, criticism or complaint by children or adults concerned to attribute all ills to the mother. Her own perspective was not there to be appreciated in its own right. Rather she was called on as the supporting cast, the embodiment of an explanation of how something had gone right or, as was often the case, gone wrong for one of the main actors.

Glenn (1994) drawing on the work of Kaplan, points to the ways in which ideology surrounding motherhood can incorporate complex and often contradictory elements. The mother is romanticized as self-sacrificing, life-giving and forgiving while simultaneously being demonized as smothering, overinvolved and destructive. Mothers are represented both as enormously powerful in the way that they can shape their children's future and therefore society, and also powerless in that they are at the mercy of the dictates of nature, instinct and social forces which they do not understand. Kaplan (1992: 48) tracing the representation of mothers in popular culture, points to three main mother paradigms: the all-sacrificing angel in the house, the overindulgent mother who is really satisfying her own needs, and the evil, possessive, all-devouring one.

The mother's responsibilities and proximity to her children have always made and continue to make her a prime suspect when things are seen to go wrong, and those who come to the conclusion that she is culpable, frequently treat her as if she is the children's sole environment, their only influence (Woollett and Phoenix 1991). Explanations for problems experienced by children tend to be overwhelmingly individualistic (Mayall 1996) and writers of all political persuasions have long since found mother-blaming a satisfactory device for explaining individual and collective misfortune: mothers are seen to hand on misery to both women and men through their mothering (Bortolaia Silva 1996).

While many of these attitudes may not have changed, since the beginning of the 1980s a sociological and historical literature has been developed by feminist scholars who have taken a different approach. These writers have focused on motherhood as a subject in two major ways. First, they have interrogated and challenged many notions about motherhood and mothering that had hitherto been regarded as self-evident, given or natural. They have considered instead how they may be understood as the 'possible outcome of specific social processes that have a historical and cultural location that can be mapped' (Smart 1996: 37). Second, some have undertaken research which attributes primacy to women's explanations and understandings of what it means to be a mother and what is involved in mothering and motherhood (e.g. Graham 1982, 1984, 1993b; Morris 1992). By placing mothers in the centre, this work has not only been more appreciative of their position and experience, but has provided a critical analysis of what went before, including work undertaken by earlier feminists.

The legacy of psychoanalysis

It has been well-documented that Freudian theory and its derivatives have left a lasting mark on western countries since awareness of them began to be felt in the 1920s (Badinter 1981; Riley 1983). In the post-Second World War period, psychodynamic understandings of the nature of human development, the language of the unconscious, masculinity and femininity, motherhood and fatherhood and the relations between children and their parents were absorbed in one form or another by significant sectors of the professions of psychiatry, child psychology and social work. Such was the impact of Freud and the post-Freudians in the United States that it has sometimes been described as a psychoanalytic deluge. By comparison, what went on in Britain may have been more of a drizzle, but the influence was substantial nevertheless (Sheldon 1994). It also had a significant influence in some areas of research, including that on mothering. For example, Graham (1977), reviewing research undertaken in the 1960s and 1970s on women's attitudes to conception and childbearing, concludes that a large percentage of in-depth studies had a psychoanalytic orientation. The effect that this and allied theories had on the dominant ways of perceiving the disabled child's family life have already been discussed in Chapter 1.

Psychoanalysis or notions derived from it did not, however, remain in the fairly limited environments of the child guidance clinic, the analyst's consulting room and the academic journal or conference. It was also popularized so that the language and some of the main tenets, albeit in a reductionist or distorted form, became ubiquitous, familiar and usable concepts in everyday life. They could be taken as givens in women's magazines, on radio, in film, theatre and literature and among professionals and policy makers who may never have so much as opened a book on Freud or his followers.

It has sometimes been argued that the real psychoanalysts could not be held responsible for what was done with their work, the way that it was popularized and the effect that this had on women in North America and Western Europe in the post-war period. Badinter (1981) and Riley (1983) refute this. They point to the part psychoanalysts themselves played in the popularization process: producing accessible texts on childrearing and child development, giving lectures and having regular slots on radio. Winnicott's (1964) text, *The Child, the Family and the Outside World*, provides one such example. Badinter (1981: 274) has this to say of psychoanalysts' enterprise in France and Britain:

> We know that Freud on several occasions refused to give advice to parents, arguing that all forms of child-rearing met with failure. In the postwar period a number of his disciples forgot the warning and moved from the descriptive to the normative. Psychoanalysts have acquired fame and fortune by sketching the portrait of the good mother and by giving advice to women through the mass media or in books written especially for them. The success of these first popularizations of psychoanalytic theory was and is sufficient proof of the confusion felt by mothers and their belief in an ideal – contradictions of the idea that maternal behaviour is instinctive. The mother's every move was subject to corrective prescription.

In some senses this can be seen as a particular version of a more general historical trend observed by Smart (1996: 46). The rules of good mothering and the ideals of good motherhood are scrutinized by experts and the demands placed on mothers increased and extended in scope:

> These rules can be seen in Foucaultian terms as the calibrations of good motherhood. Initially they covered mainly physical matters of diet, warmth, immediate environment and physical development. Later these calibrations were extended to include the immense realm of psychological care and nurture of the child. Thus the good mother was no longer simply the one who fed and cleansed properly, she would be inadequate if she failed to love *properly* and to express love in the *correct* fashion.

In the post-war years, some of the exponents of psychoanalysis and its derivatives had a number of specific and prescriptive messages to send out about the nature of mothering and motherhood. It was increasingly emphasized that the future mental health and well-being of the children rested on the nature of their early relationship with the natural mother. When that early relationship was not as it should be, problems could almost be guaranteed later in the form of delinquency or mental ill-health of some description (e.g. Bowlby 1951). Bowlby's concept of maternal deprivation, whether in the form he had intended or not, was highly influential (Rutter 1972). It has to be remembered that here we are not talking in a generalized or commonplace way about the desirability of a close and supportive relationship between mothers and children. The nature of the mother–child dyad was being defined and prescribed according to a very explicit set of theoretical understandings which have not been without their detractors.

For many, then, the absolute centrality of that early relationship between the birth mother and child *in a particular, prescribed form* became accepted wisdom, as did the dangers of being deprived of it. The stakes, then, could appear very high. If a mother did not get it right, the implication was that she could cause untold damage to her child. To succeed was difficult, however, as the projected standards for the nature of that relationship could be stringent and were apparently often deemed universally applicable.

By way of example, Badinter (1981) indicates how Winnicott defined the 'ordinary devoted mother' by her capacity to become totally submerged in and preoccupied with her child to the exclusion of any other interest. It was said to be this total immersion that ensured the child's healthy development. The mother must be ready, waiting and unhurried, attentive to her child's every need and completely and exclusively devoted. Not only must she do this, but to be successful, she must take pleasure and joy in it, too. Rather extraordinary devotion, Badinter suggests, was being redefined as something essential but ordinary. If it was ordinary, should not every woman be encouraged and expected to do it?

It may well have been that in the post-war period, some from within psychoanalysis had a genuine and benign wish to raise the status of motherhood and to support women to do something that they regarded as important and creative. Winnicott's evident enthusiasm probably wins him a place in that category (1964). It should also be recognized that within the field of psychoanalysis, there was variation in belief about the degree to which full-time mothering, at home by the child's birth mother, was essential. Nevertheless, in some quarters the idealization of what was allegedly normal mothering could make it difficult for mere mortals to succeed even in the best of circumstances – and of course many, many women were living in far from the best of circumstances. No matter how hard a woman tried, failure to make the grade could be felt to have disastrous consequences.

As Badinter (1981) has pointed out, once some of the basic ideas had been absorbed into the system and promoted by experts, there was for a while at least in some quarters, very little critical discussion of much of what was regarded as very a prestigious school of theory. Anyway, only those who were insiders and devotees of the system were seen as qualified to comment. If a woman baulked too obviously at the ideas, she could easily find herself the subject of disapproval.

While the impact of psychoanalytic ideas was undoubtedly felt in the West, it also has to be recognized that because of circumstances, necessity or inclination, many women were either unaware of or quietly disregarded both the more extreme suggestions about the ways that they should conduct their lives and the conclusions drawn by others about the consequences for them and their children if they did not conform.

By the 1960s, however, there were some women, initially in the United States, who felt that it was time to issue a formal challenge to this body of theory and the effect it was seen to have had on women. The work of Friedan (1963) and Millett (1970) provides two of the earlier examples. Friedan pointed to the way that among other things, the Freudian legacy in the post-war US meant that women were predominantly defined as homemakers and mothers. While being accepted as a woman was contingent upon having these credentials and not aspiring to anything else, being a mother left a woman horribly exposed to being blamed for almost anything that went wrong in her sons' and daughters' lives. Arguing that women's subordinacy is socially and politically constructed, Millett mounted an attack on the very cornerstones of Freudian theory and the way it characterized feminine psychopathology. Others in a strengthening women's movement followed suit, questioning what they had been told that they should be. They began to argue that they were within their rights to stake out for women having needs and interests separate and distinct from those of their children. While some feminists later engaged with psychoanalysis once again (for example, Mitchell 1974; O'Connor and Ryan 1993), they attempted to do so in a way informed by a then more established feminist politics and theory.

In the 1960s and 1970s as the established wisdom began to be challenged and as a new generation of both Marxist and feminist academics, writers and activists came to the fore, motherhood and mothers once again found themselves not the flavour of the time in some quarters. Some of the worst effects of popularized neo-Freudian ideas may have come under attack, but this did not guarantee any respite from scrutiny and criticism for mothers bringing up children and for the state of motherhood.

Mothers as reproducers of the dominant social order

Within much of the Marxism of the 1960s and 1970s, debates on the nuclear family centred on the major part that it was seen to play in maintaining a dominant social order that was oppressive to the majority. It was regarded as the site of the reproduction of labour power. Consequently mothers, by virtue of their responsibilities in relation to children, participated in ideological reproduction and transmitted the culture of state capitalism. If capitalism was to be overthrown, something needed to be done about the nuclear family and those within it.

A somewhat related debate was also occurring within feminist scholarship and we see the beginnings of an uncomfortable relationship between the women's movement and mothers and motherhood. Glenn (1994) suggests that the great divide that was to develop among feminists over motherhood reflected a basic fault line running through the history of feminism. This fault line, she suggests, centres around the question, 'What do feminists want?' She goes on to argue that some feminists, at some points, have wished to minimize the significance of sex differences and claim rights on the basis of sameness with men. Others have wished to claim a special and different identity for women, validate women's culture and move forward on the basis of those perceived commonalities.

Everingham (1994) draws attention to the way that mothering was viewed by some of the second-wave feminists of the 1960s and 1970s as a major obstacle to equality and autonomy for women. The woman's position of subordination was closely associated with her mothering role. Her only chance of achieving equality was seen to be through breaking the ties that bound her. The distinction was drawn between the essentially biological functions of pregnancy and birth and the subsequent, socially determined activities of mothering. It was in the interests of patriarchy to confuse the two and in the interests of the liberation of women to separate them (Firestone 1972; Badinter 1981).

There was more however. It was not just that mothering and motherhood restricted the woman who was mother. The ramifications were held to be much wider and more insidious than this. Were she to stay in this private, domestic sphere, she would not only not have the power to shape things herself, she would also be party to reinforcing cultural values which were defined by men and by patriarchal institutions. In other words, mothers were seen to be participating in maintaining the very institutions and gendered social relations that were contrary to their own and other women's interests. The nuclear family was one of the main sites where gendered identities were reproduced and mothers played their part in ensuring the continued oppression of women. Treblicot (1983: 1) summarizes:

> The mothering typical of patriarchies helps to perpetuate hierarchical societal arrangements in a variety of ways: women are required to give birth only to children of their own race; mothers are required to make children conform to the gender roles according to biological sex; mothers

are expected to transmit the values of the dominant culture, whatever they may be, to their children, and more generally, to teach their children to be obedient participants in hierarchy; and women are expected not only to reproduce patriarchy in children but also to care for the men who create and maintain it.

'Motherhood', Allen (1981: 315) argued, 'is dangerous to women because it continues the structure within which females must be women and mothers and conversely because it denies to females the creation of a subjectivity and worth that is open and free'.

The work of Chodorow (1978) also proved influential among some feminists. It dealt more specifically with the ways in which she saw mothers being responsible for passing on to their daughters the very attributes that would ensure that they, unlike the sons, would in turn become the nurturers. Relying on psychoanalytic theory, she argued that the mother–daughter relationship should be regarded as the key to reproducing women who would take on the same functions as their mothers.

Chodorow's (1978) work and the interest paid to it can be seen as part of a wider revival of interest in psychoanalysis among some feminists in the 1970s (e.g. Mitchell 1974). While Chodorow's work was popular in some quarters, it also generated discomfort and criticism on the part of others. Bart (1983) for example, is generally concerned about what she views as Chodorow's uncritical approach to psychoanalysis as well as the possibilities that her work opens up for mother-blaming. Glenn (1994) notes the spate of associated writing by feminists about their experience as daughters. She observes a tendency to yearn for the perfect mother while blaming their own for falling short of perfection. She suggests that many of these personal accounts reflect a belief in the all-powerful mother and the isolated mother–child dyad that is remarkably similar to more conservative views of mothering.

Benn (1998: 210–12) also comments on the 'flamboyant and ferocious tone' adopted by some feminists of the 1970s as they delivered polemics on mothers, motherhood and the tyranny of the biological family. Citing Firestone's *Dialectic of Sex* (1972) and Greer's somewhat caricatured descriptions of mothering and motherhood in *The Female Eunuch* (Greer 1971: 251–3), she concludes:

> As I have already argued, feminism's great works of the past have always been a form of 'writing against', writing against the assumption that motherhood is all that women can do. The politics of the second wave built on that older feminist view that motherhood was an essentially restricting situation, a problem that needed solving. Greer and Firestone, both published in the early 1970s, carried this 'writing against' to new heights. The new emphasis on individual creativity and self-expression, so characteristic of the sixties, and the corresponding rejection of much more deep-rooted ideas of service and love-as-work, only fuelled their disrespect for the mother of yore and lore.

Aside from concerns about the amount of vitriol and disrespect flung in the direction of mothers, there have also been debates about how satisfactory or complete were some sociological and sociopsychological accounts of the transmission of gendered identities through the family, including those by the feminists of the 1970s. Riley (1983: 3) argues:

> But while feminist work has done a tremendous amount to drag prob-lems of fertility control, maternity and sexual choice away from the clutch of received opinion about the 'natural', we cannot subside con-tentedly at this point. Any feminist-influenced political philosophy would have to commit itself to a more profound re-examination of nature and culture than is given by reiterating the usual corrective to biologism, the claim for the 'social construction' of reality. For this only substitutes an unbounded sphere of social determination for that of bio-logical determination. If we are to talk the language of social construc-tions, then the construction of the very concepts of the social and the biological must also be elucidated.

Morgan (1996) also suggests that such analyses offer an overdeterminist picture which is not particularly good at accounting for change in the gender order. In addition, he argues, they are not especially effective at assessing the part played by other institutions in the construction of gendered identities.

The work undertaken by second-wave feminists of the 1960s and 1970s was, of course, extremely important. Among other things they unhooked the biological from the social and opened up the debate about the structural dimensions of the problems faced by women, problems that had hitherto been regarded as personal and individual in the narrowest sense. They politicized the domestic, the private and the personal. They gave a sense of the enormous barriers ranged against women and helped to legitimate wishes, aspirations and activities that had previously been regarded as off-limits. They acknow-ledged the costs to women of things routinely expected of them as mothers and highlighted the fact that frequently children's needs were met only because women supressed some of their own needs. Like Marxists (and some, of course, were both Marxist and feminist) they also gained a sense of how we can all unwittingly participate in and collude with our own downfall by incor-porating ideology that is in neither our own interest nor that of those we love most.

Having said that, many did not serve mothers or motherhood too fairly or too well. While none should underestimate the power of dominant ideology (never mind material constraints and much else besides), there is a sense in some analyses of the mother being presented merely as a conduit through which ideological discourse flows as she passively reproduces labour power or gendered identities. She participates in teaching her children things that are not necessarily in their interests and frequently not in her own either. We are given no sense of someone able to experience and deal with uncomfortable contradictions, no sense of her discriminating between what is good, bad or indifferent for herself or her child. She is blissfully unaware or, if she gets an inkling, unable to act. In all of this there is rarely any feeling of the mother as an active agent challenging anything or putting her stamp on the proceedings in any way other than that prescribed by the dominant social order. The model has within it no strong sense of the possibility of mothers' questioning, rebelling or resisting. There is rarely, if ever, a whiff of irreverent disregard for the status quo. No feeling here of their cocking a snook and finding some elbow room for themselves and their children. The prospect presented was overwhelmingly dire.

No small wonder then, if some feminists began to question whether this was how they wanted to see the world of women, mothers and motherhood. A faultline in feminism began to show in sharp relief. As Glenn (1994) has argued, there were many feminists reluctant to write off or give up the idea of mothering as something special. Some writers, perhaps those who began to experience motherhood for themselves (as opposed to viewing it from the recalled perspective of their own childhoods), found that the relationship with a child could be thrilling in unanticipated ways. Some, having tried the world of work, possibly discovered that it was not always all it was cracked up to be. Having a child seemed a satisfying alternative option or parallel development. Alienation in the public sphere, Glenn suggests, may have been one of the factors which led feminists to want to reinstate the family, children and motherhood as sites of personal satisfaction. For those working-class women, who had always combined mothering and much else besides with low-paid, manual work outside the home, it would have come as no surprise that the workplace was unlikely to provide personal fulfilment (Pollert 1981).

It has also been suggested (Benn 1998: 212) that feminism (or perhaps some dominant voices within it) had ignored what many women had known all along:

> But this left another story untold, an important side of women's experience unexpressed. For motherhood is not *only* drudgery. Being a mother is calming; it is moving; it is enlightening; it is fun. These ordinary pleasures seem so obvious to most women. For them, their enjoyment or, at least their acceptance of their own parenthood is not just a collapse into private life, a refusal to take up a challenge. It is a different *sort* of challenge, a place where a variety of values can be expressed and maintained. To create and rear a human being can be a fundamental expression of the most positive of human qualities: love. And yes: love-as-work. While feminism's boldest and best story – and certainly its most publicised one – has always been the tale of the one who got away, it has always had a slight difficulty with the one who stayed behind and *liked* it.

Just as many women had only been affected in a diluted form by the trickle-down effect of psychoanalysis, it is unlikely that any more than a minority were even aware of the debates on motherhood that were taking place within the women's movement. For the majority, the idea of finding salvation through the rejection of motherhood and the dismantling of the nuclear family was never an option that they considered.

Motherhood, when different is good

A reformed view of mothers and mothering, which began to emerge within the women's movement in the late 1970s and 1980s, has to be seen in the context of what Benn (1998) calls 'difference feminism'. In contrast to what had gone before, some began to reassess and value interests, attitudes, behaviours and ways of thinking that were seen to be characteristic of many women. Everingham (1994) describes how women began to challenge some of the central notions which had inspired the second wave, questioning whether they were male constructs and values that were being pursued at the expense of other values of nurturance commonly associated with women and, of course, mothering.

Benn gives the example of Friedan's *The Second Stage* (1981). For a range of reasons, not least because of its re-embracing of the family, this book had a distinctly unfriendly reception from some other feminists at the time. Benn points out, however, that in her formulation of 'family-friendly' feminism, Friedan merely anticipated much of what would develop in the mainstream of the movement during the decade that followed: 'Friedan understood that there are all sorts of human effort, that effort of career is not the only effort worth making nor the only success by which we should judge ourselves' (Benn 1998: 226).

The work of other American writers such as Gilligan (1982), Belenky *et al.* (1986) and Ruddick (1989) was both influential in shaping feminist thought and responsive to the changing pulse of the time. Writers such as these sought to describe and value what women typically were and what they typically did. They proposed that in many respects, women had different capacities from men and worked within an alternative ethical framework. They argued, however, that this different moral system was valid and essential and demanded equal respect to that followed by men. Traditional nurturant qualities commonly associated with mothering were to be celebrated.

Ruddick (1989) projects mothering as a highly creative, philosophical and rational discipline in its own right. The mother has a particular and crucial part to play in her children's development. Rather than merely transmitting what has been required of her, she has the opportunity to pass on her own values to the child.

Everingham (1994) gives an account of the way that such views were castigated for being 'maternal revivalism' and conservative, patriarchal family values by another name. Some critics argued that this notion of the mother's role simply reinforced the elaborate charade that women had agency and control over their lives in ways that they did not. Could it be that this was just another example of glorified self-negation by women? Others were uncomfortable with the possibility that this romanticized motherhood and mothering.

Perhaps it is inevitable that a little idealization goes on once groups which have suffered from being negatively defined by others seize the chance to redefine themselves. After all, in Socialist Realist art, all workers have noble profiles! It may have been tempting (and possibly irksome) for a while at least to project and overplay the stereotype of the Wise Woman, but such treatment of motherhood was reasonably short-lived in most places where it happened. The revalidation of motherhood and mothering, however, was much more lasting and there was a significant expansion of interest in the subject among women writers in the late 1980s and 1990s. The growing recognition among feminist writers of the significance of difference and diversity (e.g. Hirsh and Fox Keller 1990) also provided a fertile context for future work on motherhood.

Mothers in their own right

A number of strong and overlapping themes emerge from work on mothering and motherhood in the 1980s and 1990s and in this section, I shall concentrate on three of them. The first concerns efforts to enable women who are mothers to have a voice, to give their own accounts of their lives and to be taken seriously while doing it. The second deals with a strengthening focus on the importance of recognizing diversity and the consequences for some women when this is neglected. The third theme is about characterizing the mother as an active agent and challenging the view of her simply as the passive conduit for the values of others.

By the beginning of the 1980s, a strong 'let the people speak' trend had already become quite well-established in some areas of social science research. Some of this work adopted an ethnographic approach to investigating people's lives, utilizing forms of enquiry which involved the researcher becoming steeped in the detail of the daily round of the subjects of research while attending to their accounts of their experience and learning from their interpretations (e.g. Willis 1978; Corrigan 1979; Pollert 1981). Other writers, using variants of the interview as their standard research tool, also sought to place the understandings offered by the subjects at the very heart of what they did (e.g. Graham 1977, 1980, 1984; Glendinning 1983). When, as was frequently the case, the people who were the subjects of such research were members of some of the least powerful groups in society, their understandings often stood in sharp contrast to other, more dominant views of the world.

This approach to research and writing was used effectively by some feminist scholars to investigate women's experience, including their domestic lives. Perhaps it was the fact that their work brought them face to face with the women concerned that produced such appreciative insights into their lives. The respect that the researchers developed for the women is reflected in their writing and it was no longer a case of the off-stage 'mother of yore and lore' being discussed by those who knew better. Much of the time, the researchers cast new light on the ordinary, the everyday and the commonplace. They remarked on the hitherto unremarkable.

The women who were the subjects of Pollert's (1981) research were amazed that their lives at home and on the production line in a tobacco factory were of any interest to anyone. Pollert sought to understand their consciousness, their accounts of the double burden of the sheer hard work that they managed at home and on the shop floor, the balancing and juggling of the two, the seeming impossibility of getting respite or change as well as their moments of resistance.

Some feminist work on motherhood in the early 1980s also focused on the hidden hardship in the women's lives by detailing the nature and size of the workloads that the mothers routinely carried. Graham (1980) argued that by 'listening to mother' we learn how, in hard times, such women struggle to preserve the standards of living of other members of the family by going without themselves. They act as the buffers who absorb and deflect the worst effects of economic decline and low income on those close to them. Listening to the way mothers talk about their lives, she suggests, helps to fill a theoretical vacuum by bridging the gap between the abstract analysis of feminism and those everyday experiences in women's lives that feminism tries to address.

Through listening to mothers' own accounts of motherhood and what it meant to them, writers further developed the notion of the woman as the buffer who absorbs problems and is responsible for the health of other family members (Graham 1984, 1985, 1993b; Blackburn 1991). The buck stops with her, they argue, and in the main, it is she who is held responsible and who herself accepts responsibility for protecting, maintaining and promoting health and well-being within the household. She provides care in sickness and in health. She is the sorter-out and the juggler. She often does not have control over household resources but she usually has to manage them (Pahl 1988). When there is not enough of something to go round, whether it be food, money or attention, it is likely to be the mother who makes the difficult economies, and balances the financial, material and emotional budget. She frequently does it at her own expense.

The process of giving mothers a voice in research as well as the the publication of autobiographical accounts of the experience of mothering (e.g. Gieve 1989; Morris 1992) has done much to legitimate their perspectives. In turn this has allowed comparisons to be drawn between the views of the women and those of 'experts' (e.g. Graham and Oakley 1981). Consequently a strong theme that has emerged in work on mothers and mothering has been related to the degradation of mothers' own opinions and expertise in favour of those held by 'experts' whose job it is to define how mothering shall best be done (Bortolaia Silva 1996; Smart 1996). Attention has also often been drawn to the gulf that exists between the idealized prescriptions of mothering that are sometimes to be found in childcare manuals and the daily experience of many women's lives (Woollett and Phoenix 1991). Smart (1996: 47) comments on the 'tests' routinely applied by experts to ascertain whether mothers meet or fail the standards of motherhood: 'There are now myriad ways of failing and, as the range of *expertise* on motherhood expands, so there are added new dimensions of success and failure'.

Turning to the second theme, while the commonality of some shared experiences may strike a chord for a wide variety of women, it began to be acknowledged in the 1990s that attending to mothers meant listening to women from much more diverse backgrounds than had hitherto been acknowledged.

Consequently an issue that has come to the fore has been the way in which the question of diversity has been ignored. This in many ways reflects a wider recognition of the fact that in the published word or in the formal arena of debate, the experience of some individuals and groups has been marginalized, rendered pathological or written out of the picture altogether. There has been an acknowledgement of the way in which theoreticians within feminism obscured the differences between women and masked essential dimensions of their lives (Graham 1993a; Morris 1993). Work that purported to speak of *all* women's experience was in fact frequently partial, reflecting the lives of *particular* groups or social divisions.

More specifically on motherhood, Phoenix and Woollett (1991a) point to commonalities of experience between women, particularly when they live in similar circumstances and have children of a similar age. They also emphasize, however, how varied circumstances may lead to women experiencing motherhood in diverse ways and having different understandings of what it means.

Even when attention is given to diversity, however, it is not always approached in a way that is sufficiently appreciative of the complexity of women's lives. Phoenix and Woollett (1991b) warn that even when class and race are acknowledged as variables in research, they are frequently dealt with in a way that is clumsy and unrefined, and does not recognize how these concepts encompass huge differences in circumstances and practices. They also highlight some of the consequences of this for those whose lives depart from the dominant descriptions (and prescriptions) of mothering and family life. They give the example of the ways that crude understandings can dictate and limit service provision for the women and children concerned.

Glenn (1994) has argued that while mothering is in fact a historically and culturally variable relationship, a particular definition of it has dominated popular media representations, academic discourse and political and legal doctrine. This, together with universalist assumptions, means that alternative beliefs and practices among racial, ethnic, and sexual minority communities have gone unnoticed. She further suggests that the social base of mothering becomes apparent when we attend to variations rather than searching for the universal. The history of particular groups and the social structures within which they live make sense of their approaches to mothering and show why it is different from dominant definitions.

A growing number of writers have highlighted this set of issues by focusing on particular marginalized groups. For example, the work of Graham (1982, 1993b) and Blackburn (1991) details the experiences of diverse groups of women bringing up children in poverty. By locating the women's accounts of what they do in the exacting conditions of extreme material hardship, we are enabled to understand the limitations placed upon them as well as the positive choices that they make as they raise their children. Morris (1992) brings to the fore how dominant definitions of motherhood exclude single motherhood. She points to the way that single mothers are problematized, with stigmatizing stereotypes consistently being applied to them. Gregory (1991) discusses how dominant notions of motherhood do not include the experience of mothers of deaf children. Just as their children are often excluded from the general category of children, so too are their mothers written out of the mainstream picture of mothering. Glenn (1994) traces the way that Black American women were incorporated into the United States largely to take advantage of their labour. She argues that, as a result, they were excluded from the prevalent version of the cult of domesticity that bedevilled many white women, particularly those who were not poor. Because the Black woman was there first as a slave and then as a low-wage labourer, this was seen to take precedence over her value as a mother to her own children. Despite the efforts of these and other writers, there is of course a very long way to go before the dominant descriptions (and prescriptions) of motherhood and families reflect the diverse and changing patterns of living that exist within the population as a whole.

The third and final theme to be considered is that concerned with what is often termed the agency of women as mothers. More recently, feminist writers have increasingly resisted the earlier notion of mothers being passively constructed, being agents of irresistible, dominant forces. As Kaplan (1992) points out, feminist historians have become aware of women's surprising resilience in the face of oppression and their rebelliousness against practices that cause hardship and suffering. Influenced at least in part by the work of Gilligan, Ruddick and others like them, as well as postmodernist theory (e.g. McNay 1992), a growing number of feminist writers perceive mothers as active subjects of history, shaping culture and creating cultural and moral values for themselves and others (Everingham 1994; Bortolaia Silva 1996). They are characterized as being involved in an active, rational and interpretive process which entails making sensitive, responsive and context-dependent judgements and decisions (Everingham 1994). The notion is sometimes emphasized that mothers go to considerable lengths to create whatever safe space they can to keep their children healthy and to help them grow emotionally and physically (Blackburn 1991; Morris 1992).

Mayall's (1996) work on mothering is perhaps a particularly helpful example of the way such ideas are being applied and therefore merits more detailed consideration. Exploring the types of tasks undertaken by mothers and the nature of their relationship with their mainly young children, she describes how there is a continuous and shifting balance between different activities. The relationship is constructed and reconstructed through the care of the children's bodily and emotional well-being. While the need by mothers to exercise control should not be underestimated, the giving of care, warmth and comfort is equally important, as is the more equal relationship of companionship based on shared daily experiences.

The fact that children are not passive either is viewed as important for it suggests that mothering cannot rightly be construed merely as a top-down socialization activity. Children's needs and wants are powerful in shaping and structuring the relationship. Consequently it needs to be seen as a much more interactive enterprise, requiring a great deal of collaboration between active parties in order to make something workable and worthwhile of their lives. Children and mothers, therefore, try to negotiate a reasonably comfortable daily life which accommodates both the need by mothers to exercise control and the need by children to make their voices heard. Mayall also argues that women socialize children to suit some social norms and that this is recognized by both mothers and children. While there is sometimes tension between this and other more protective and enabling activities based on attentive love, the two should not be regarded as in conflict in every way. Intrinsic to the activity of mothering, she suggests, is preparing children to face the world as it is and giving them the emotional strength to do so.

Mayall also proposes that children's relative vulnerability and lack of knowledge about certain things means that they need 'allies on the ground'. She suggests that mothers frequently adopt this role and that there is often common cause between mothers and children in the interests of the welfare of the child. The judgements that the mother makes in relation to this are derived from a morality grounded in her experience of the relationship with the child and this morality is, in turn, critical to the development of the child's learning. The closeness of the relationship means that discussions take place between them, and in that context, mothers make moral decisions and adjudications about crucial matters. Having common cause often entails mothers acting as mediators against some of the more harsh and powerful pressures on children to conform to things not in their interests. Mothers become their children's advocates formally and informally. Doing so can be enormously difficult as they are often negotiating with others in contexts where a different morality, a different view of the world, evidently holds sway.

Common cause between mother and child clearly does not mean that their needs, wants and views of the world are coterminous. There may be undeniable conflicts of interest that are difficult to resolve without mother or child feeling that they lose out temporarily or over time. In turn, analyses that focus solely or predominantly on the needs of either party often do so only at the expense of the other. The question of whose voice shall be rightly heard, whose needs define a given situation and who is the focus of concern, is a matter that has been central not only to work on children and their mothers but also to that on informal caring.

Understanding caring

Research and writing on informal caring has expanded since the beginning of the 1980s, initially as a result of the interest shown in the subject by feminist scholars. The use of the term 'care' in this context is not without its critics. There is some discomfort about the fact that by using this as a catch-all word, the emotional content or feelings in the relationship are not differentiated from the tasks that are undertaken. Some writers have felt it helpful to distinguish between 'caring for' and 'caring about' while others have tried to separate 'caring' from 'tending'. Some have argued that 'care' should never be used when it really means assistance or even control; it should be used only to mean love (Morris 1993a).

There is much in the literature on informal caring that echoes some of the debates already outlined in relation to mothering. This is not surprising in view of the fact that gendered relations within the domestic sphere have come to be regarded as central to theoretical work on the subject. Also, among feminist academics, theorizing on the provision of informal care for groups of people other than children followed on naturally from the more established debates on childcare (Twigg and Atkin 1994).

From the beginning of the 1980s there has been a substantial amount of writing on informal care, which has had as its main focus the fact that this work is primarily undertaken by women. It has been argued that terms such as 'community care' and 'care in the family' are misleading, for what is under discussion is not care by the whole of the community or the family. It is unpaid, domestic labour by women and always has been.

A great deal of writing in the 1980s concentrated on the experience of the carers, on the sheer hard work and the restrictions imposed on women by this hidden labour of love (e.g. Finch and Groves 1980; Pitkeathly 1989). Thus a debate around caring was being constructed with the oppression of women carers as its prime focus. Graham (1993a: 461) summarizes:

> Caring was defined in terms of the unpaid domestic and personal services provided through the social relations of marriage and kinship to those who, for reasons of illness or impairment, found it hard to meet their own care needs. It was a definition that focused attention on gender and on the material and ideological processes which confirmed women as carers.

In view of later criticism about the limitations of this definition, it is important to recognize how new such an approach then was. For the first time the rights and aspirations of informal carers, a particularly powerless and hidden group, were being regarded as important, worthy of consideration and worthy of a voice. Again we see feminists and other writers investigating the domestic sphere and highlighting the taken-for-granted, the implied and the invisible.

Subsequently, some of the early writing was challenged on a number of grounds. First, the assumption by many that men were rarely if ever involved in informal caring work was demonstrated to be an oversimplified view. By the end of the 1980s it was becoming clear that more men were undertaking caring tasks than had hitherto been acknowledged. It emerged, however, that it was certainly true that women were more likely to be the main carers either alone or in households with others and that they were also undertaking different types of care work (Parker and Lawton 1994). Men undertook some care, then, but it was of a different type to that offered by women and was more likely to be supplementary to that provided by the main female carer. In addition, it was found that actions that were regarded as remarkable when performed by a male carer were seen merely as an extension of a woman's normal domestic role. Service providers had lower expectations of what men should do in this respect and therefore were more likely to offer support to them than to women in comparable positions (Twigg and Atkin 1994).

In the early 1990s, it also began to be argued that feminist work on caring had become fixed in the form that had been established at the beginning of the previous decade (Graham 1993a). While feminist thought had moved on, theorizing on caring did not reflect this. The early work, it was suggested, represented the perspectives of only some women (mainly white, heterosexual women in established households) while purporting to speak of the experience of women in general. This left the experience, needs and wishes of many women marginalized or touched upon in only a crude fashion (Gunarantam 1993; Morris 1993b; Twigg and Atkin 1994; Morgan 1996).

In addition, it has been powerfully argued that earlier feminist work on caring defined disabled and older women out of the category of womankind (Morris 1993b). When the writers spoke of 'women' they meant non-disabled, not-elderly women who were providing assistance. Apart from the dehumanizing effect of this on disabled and older women, it meant that feminist work on caring had not identified or engaged with the subjective experience of those women (and men) who required personal assistance. They were definitely in the category of 'them', not 'us', with little recognition that the categories of those requiring or providing assistance and care are more fluid at any given time or over time, than is often assumed. Those needing assistance and care tended to be accorded the limited and negative role of being the burden to be shouldered by 'women'. There was too little acknowledgement of the fact that people who are themselves disabled or older often give care and assistance to others. The relationship was often characterized as being one-way and there was little sense of any possibility of reciprocity (Morris 1993b). There has also been concern, particularly from those within the disabled people's movement, about the way that what is seen as an exclusive focus on carers has deflected attention away from the rights, needs and wishes of disabled people themselves.

Alongside these critiques, there began to emerge a range of work on caring that addresses some of the limitations of previous work. Attention has been given to the nature of the relationships involved and more detailed investigation undertaken on the complexity of them. Twigg and Atkin (1994), in their review of work on caring, suggest that the concept of caring contains a number of elements. There is the performance of supportive tasks that go beyond what is normally expected, beyond the usual reciprocities. Physical labour is often involved and this can be hard and routine. They also comment on the fact that being involved in a caring relationship often entails strong feelings of responsibility on the part of the carer. Carers frequently have a sense that the buck stops with them and they have to ensure that things are made to happen, including the provision of essential services by outside organizations.

Co-residence is significant in the construction of caring relationships, as is kinship and its associated obligations. Most informal care is bound up with and grows out of established kinship relations; because of particular characteristics, events or circumstances, a social, familial relationship is translated into an informal caring relationship. Finch (1989: 242) also points out that studies from carers' perspectives typically reflect their view of caring relationships with kin that are determined by a mixture of 'love, duty, affection and obligation'. However, she adds:

In reality, the 'sense of obligation' which marks the distinctive character of kin relationships is nothing like its image in political debate, where it appears as a set of ready-made rules which all right-thinking people accept and put into practice. It is actually much less reliable than that. It is nurtured and grows over time between some individuals more than others, and its practical consequences are highly variable. It does have a binding quality but that derives from commitments built up between real people over many years, not from an abstract set of moral values.

She also highlights the importance of the notion of reciprocity within family assistance and the way that such obligations build up over time. Individuals, particularly if they are children, are not always expected to give back directly to the person who gives to them. There is a more complex balance sheet with people doing their bit in different ways. Children, for example, may be assumed to be receiving substantially from their parents but may only be expected to pay back to the next generation.

Caring is also closely associated with emotion. Caring relations, Twigg and Atkin (1994: 8) suggest 'if not defined by love, are frequently associated with and energized by it, although in more complex and ambiguous ways than the normative picture might suggest'. Love underwrites the 'bonds of obligation', explaining *why* people undertake caring as well as the *way* that caring is experienced – but emotion is seen to be a significant element in a different way, too. Caring is itself a form of emotional labour in that carers do not simply do tasks for people. The personal support, encouragement, attention and conversation that they offer is an additional and integral part of the relationship.

Morgan (1996) argues that within caring relationships, a woman gives emotion at least as much as any kind of physical labour. The role involves a multiplicity of skills, as she is expected to handle the emotions of others, smooth tensions between other family members and provide a refuge from and counterbalance to the strains of the public sphere. The recognition of unpaid 'emotional labour' as substantial and significant allows us to acknowledge the expenditure of effort and personal resources within the domestic sphere as real work. Morgan also suggests that the idea of emotional labour can be extended to the person defined as being in receipt of care. People have to work at being ones who are cared for. Things are expected of them and they have to cope as much as the carers, albeit in very different ways.

Since the early 1990s, there has been an expansion in work by disabled people themselves which has countered the one-sided frame of reference in earlier work (Begum 1990; Morris 1991, 1993b; Begum *et al.* 1994). The negative consequences of relying on informal care or assistance from family and friends have been explicated and some have argued strongly that whenever possible, it is in the interests of everyone for the necessary resources to be placed under the control of the disabled people themselves. By such means they may be enabled to determine what they require in the way of personal assistance and purchase it accordingly. They may also be released from the 'burden of gratitude' (Begum 1990) and have the opportunity to have reciprocal relationships with those close to them that are not distorted by the demands of informal care and by the emotional labour intrinsic to it.

We have also seen an extension of the range of research giving attention to the diversity in populations of those involved in giving informal care. As a result, there is now more information than before about the experiences of groups of carers who were neglected or marginalized, particularly those from minority ethnic communities and those on low incomes (Baxter *et al*. 1990; Begum 1992; Butt and Mirza 1996). It is increasingly recognized that for some in the population, the giving and receiving of informal care and assistance is a harsher and more restrictive experience because of poverty and social and geographical exclusion (Graham 1993a).

Concluding comments

Mothers of disabled children can be seen as both mothers and as part of the population of informal carers more generally. A binding and caring relationship grows from a parent–child involvement but often extends beyond the time of childhood. While many parents and their children may feel a close tie that lasts a lifetime, few are bound together as intimately as many of the mothers and their disabled sons and daughters.

This chapter has shown the strong influence in the post-war period of a number of theoretical perspectives that have been brought to bear on motherhood and mothering. Not all of these have been particularly appreciative of women-as-mothers. We have seen, however, how more recent work has sought to put the women as subjects and their perspectives centre stage. It has developed more positive analyses of their lives and of what they try to achieve. Such approaches offer a view of mothers as more active subjects in the social contexts in which they live and operate. They work within perceived constraints in order to try to shape individuals, events and circumstances. I shall suggest in Chapter 6 that this more recent theoretical work can illuminate the experience of the West Midlands mothers and others like them who bring up disabled children.

Just as ways of theorizing motherhood have not been uncontested, the same can also be said of work on informal caring more generally. I also considered in this chapter how theoretical work on disablement that is both feminist and sociologically-based has been influential in questioning assumptions about informal caring that had become established across the 1980s. Among other things, such an approach has alerted us to the dangers of the way that a narrow and exclusive focus on the opinions, needs and wishes of carers may dehumanize those who require assistance. In the next chapter, I shall consider in greater detail changes in the way that disability has come to be theorized in the 1980s and 1990s and the ways that disabled people have been active in redefining themselves and their experience. I shall then consider the implications that this has for the views expressed by the mothers about the place that their disabled children occupy in the world.

 **5**

Living in a hostile context

In the previous chapter, I considered some of the ways in which mothering, motherhood and caring have been theorized. At times, as we have seen, the mother's perspectives and her expert knowledge about this aspect of her own life was left to one side. We also saw that some of the work that attempted to redress that balance and to give women's interests and perspectives a more central place has been criticized for marginalizing those for whom the women provided care and assistance. It is suggested that they were frequently seen as burdens to be shouldered in literature that characterized the caring relationship in particular ways and heard only the voices of those defined as the carers. The discrimination and oppression experienced by those who required care and assistance was neglected.

In this chapter, I turn to discrimination and oppression faced by disabled children and adults. Such experience is of course important in its own right but in addition, the recognition of its impact on their children was one of the things that drove the actions of the West Midlands mothers. They and those in other studies had had experiences that led them to believe that their sons and daughters were living in a world which in some respects at least, had shown itself to be discriminatory towards disabled children and hostile to their interests. As Traustadottir (1991) observed in relation to other such mothers, their concerns were not limited to their own children and to the specific events that had had a negative impact upon them. The experience of having a disabled child had heightened their awareness of the position of disabled children and adults more generally. For example, when some of the West Midlands mothers saw a news item about children and their families having an unhappy experience at the hands of others, for some there was undoubtedly a strong sense of identification and a feeling of 'there but for the grace of God'. Similarly, they expressed anger or concern about policy matters which may not have affected them directly but which were having an impact on people whom they saw as being *like* them in some way or another, people on their side of the track.

At the time of my discussions with the West Midlands mothers, their sons and daughters had all either reached adulthood or were nearing it. They had experienced the upbringing of a disabled child but the world of disabled adults was also of immediate relevance to them. The position of disabled adults is a matter of crucial interest to parents of much younger children too. Children and childhood are of course important in their own right but parents are also acutely aware that their young sons and daughters are adults-in-the-making. When they see something positive or negative happening to a disabled adult, they may well ask themselves whether that is what the world has in store for their child later on.

The purpose of this chapter is to locate in a broader context the West Midlands mothers' belief that, in the past 20 years, they had experienced many aspects of contemporary life that were hostile to their sons' and daughters' interests and those of others like them. They raised questions about discriminatory attitudes that they regarded as prevalent not only among lay people but among some professionals too. They spoke of services that were thin on the ground and based on misguided assumptions. They raised concerns about exclusionary arrangements and practices that limited their sons and daughters and prevented them from doing things that others took for granted. Some spoke of their concern that standards and practices that would not be tolerated for a non-disabled child were regarded as acceptable for their disabled children. The mothers had found themselves having to challenge the unacceptable in the interests of their sons' and daughters' well-being.

A number of the mothers also volunteered that they had seen positive progress during this period and commented that issues related to disability were now discussed much more openly and frequently than in the past. A number were very appreciative of those practitioners whom they regarded as providing a service of quality to themselves and their children.

When we consider the now substantial British literature that is concerned with the disadvantage, discrimination and oppression experienced by disabled children and adults, we find a great deal in it that reflects the concern and unease of the women in the study. Much of this literature has developed during the lifetime of the young adults whose mothers were interviewed and has challenged many of the things that the women saw as troubling.

In this chapter, I want only to summarize a number of the recurring themes which can be found in this rapidly expanding literature. First, I shall consider ways in which disability is defined and theorized and I shall look at how the concept of diversity has come to be seen as significant and central. I shall describe the ways in which disabled people have routinely been subjected to dehumanization, devaluation and exclusion by a number of means and I shall review some of the damaging and oppressive dimensions of service provision. Finally, in keeping with the experience and expressed views of the West Midlands mothers, I shall refer to some of the positive change that has been taking place in recent years.

The development of theories of discrimination and oppression

During the past two decades, a growing number of writers in Britain have given voice to a developing set of understandings which have challenged more established and dominant explanations of disablement. More particularly, in the 10 years between the mid–1980s and 1990s, a number of disabled writers and activists have produced a sociologically-based set of analyses of the situation of disabled people that has had a significant impact (Abberley 1996).

At the end of the 1970s and through the first part of the 1980s, more theoretical work began to appear which drew attention to the fragile position occupied by disabled people within the social structure (e.g. UPIAS 1976; Finkelstein 1980; Ryan and Thomas 1980; Shearer 1980, 1984; Walker 1980; Campling 1981; Sutherland 1981; Thomas 1982; Tomlinson 1982; Oliver 1983, 1985; Leonard 1984; Hannaford 1985; Abberley 1987; Barton 1987; Read 1987). What this undeniably varied work had in common, was that it did not see the disadvantaged position of disabled people as natural, inevitable or acceptable. It attempted to account for it theoretically and began to challenge whether the state of affairs that existed need always remain.

At the end of the 1970s and the first half of the 1980s, then, we see established a tradition of writing on disability by both disabled and non-disabled people, which has at its core a strong political dimension. In such work, the relationship between matters hitherto regarded as private troubles and those defined as public or structural issues is seen to be intimate and complex. An assumption is frequently explicated that all of our most personal and individual experiences are informed one way or another by the material, social and economic places that we occupy within the wider social structure and by the identity, power and value accorded to the groups to which we are seen to belong.

A further feature of the emerging approach was that it validated the subjective experience of disabled people more strongly than ever before. The documenting of their experience informed developing theory on the problems that they faced. It also enabled them to redefine and represent their lives in ways that ran counter to dominant and orthodox accounts (e.g. Hannaford 1985; Saxton and Howe 1988; Morris 1989).

Central to a very great deal of the literature on disability that was to develop over the 1980s and 1990s was the notion that some of the most restricting and debilitating features in the lives of disabled children and adults are not necessary or inevitable consequences of having impairments. It was persistently argued that many of these restricting features are social constructions and can therefore be changed by social and political means. As a consequence, the locus of the definition of problems experienced by disabled children and adults was being shifted from the purely private and individual to the domain of public, social and civil rights. Disabled people began to be understood as a marginalized group experiencing discrimination and oppression. Within this literature the language of restricting impairments and disabling medical conditions gives way to the language of human and civil rights and citizenship (e.g. Barton 1996; Oliver 1996; Morris 1998). Disabled children and adults are characterized less as patients or people in need of help and more as disenfranchised citizens, denied the civil, social and legal rights which others take for granted (Barnes 1991; Bynoe *et al.* 1991; Gooding 1994). Disabled people are seen to be excluded, by both crude and subtle means, from creating and participating in a shared political and social heritage. They are prevented from living their lives according to prevailing standards enjoyed by their nondisabled peers (Oliver 1996).

There had, of course, been earlier and very distinguished work in the 1970s which explicitly recognized the significance of social factors in relation to disablement (e.g. Blaxter 1976). In the early 1980s, some had culminated in the World Health Organization's International Classification of Impairments, Diseases and Handicaps (WHO 1980). This work marked an important and major departure from understandings of disability that concentrated solely on disease, disorder and defect, and admitted a sociomedical model that reflected to a greater degree, the social content and consequences of disablement (Baldwin and Carlisle 1994; Bury 1996). A distinction was made between the impairment (a perceived abnormality in the body's structure or function), the disability (the restriction in ability to perform tasks seen as normal) and the handicap (the social disadvantage related to impairment or disability). This approach was further developed for use in the OPCS surveys of disabled children and adults which were undertaken in the United Kingdom in the mid- and late 1980s (Bury 1996).

Despite this changing emphasis and the greater attention paid to restrictions imposed by social conditions, these and related approaches were challenged by disabled academics whose work within the expanding field of disabilities studies both reflected and informed the growing disabled people's movement of the 1980s and 1990s (e.g. Abberley 1992; Oliver 1996). From among the ranks of this steadily growing number of disabled writers there emerged a major paradigm shift and the development of variants of what came to be known as the 'social model of disability' (Oliver 1983, 1990, 1996; Abberley 1987; Morris 1991; Barnes 1997). This was not just a matter of acknowledging social effects, social contexts or discriminatory treatment experienced by disabled people. Rather, the disabled theorists and activists of the 1980s and 1990s were fundamentally redefining disability as the social restriction, oppression and disadvantage experienced by people who had impairments. Disability was seen to be socially created and extrinsic to the individual. It has sometimes been suggested that impairment refers to the physical, sensory or intellectual limitations of function while disability explains the social, economic and political experiences associated with it (Morris 1994). It was argued by some that fundamental to the social model was an insistence that there was no causal relationship between impairment and disability (Oliver 1996). Along with the development and incorporation of the social model by the disabled people's movement, came the strong rejection of medical or individual models which conceptualized disability as a personal attribute or problem (Oliver 1990, 1996).

Abberley (1996: 65) has pointed to the significance of the relationship between the disabled people's movement and those disabled academics developing a sociological analysis of disability between the mid-1980s and mid-1990s:

> However, this advance would not have been possible if it were only occurring in the minds of isolated individuals. Intimately involved in the genesis of these works is a real movement of disabled people in Britain, and the force of academic work resides to a large degree in the fact that they crystallize within them the beliefs, concerns and interests of the increasing number of disabled people who themselves see disablement as a social process rather than a personal tragedy, some of whom reject all negative evaluations of impairment.

Intrinsic to the work of these disabled academics was also an alternative vision of what might be and a focus on matters which they believed could be changed in order to make that vision a reality (Oliver 1990; Morris 1991; Abberley 1996). Out of a close engagement of the academic and political movements came the conviction on the part of some that the primary purpose of disability research and theory was to serve the liberation and emancipation of disabled people as they, themselves, collectively defined it (Oliver 1992; Abberley 1997).

While there are unifying elements within this tradition of disability theory, there are, as would be expected, a range of perspectives that reflect both developments within the wider field of social theory and the life experience and identities of different groups and individuals from within the population of disabled people. Barnes (1997) identifies the materialist position underpinning some of the original work on the social model by writers such as Oliver (1983, 1990) and Finkelstein (1980). He indicates the way that the approach that they established has been criticized by other disabled writers for its neglect of the individual experience of disabled people with reference to gender, minority ethnic status and impairment (e.g. Morris 1991; French 1993; Stuart 1993; Begum *et al* 1994; Crow 1996). He points to theoretical developments within the field of disability studies influenced by feminist and postmodernist scholarship and the growth in attention to culture and cultural representation (Shakespeare 1994).

As Barnes's account indicates, the question of impairment and how it should be seen has proved troubling to a number of disabled and non-disabled writers, all of whom recognize the debilitating impact of hostile material and ideological environments upon disabled people. Further, some disabled activists and writers, who regard the social model itself as one of the most significant liberational influences in disabled people's lives, are neverthless uneasy about the way that impairment is sometimes character-ized within it. This makes it crucial to consider debates about the place of impairment within a social theory of disability. As Barnes also recognizes, the significance attributed to diversity of experience and origin also merits attention.

The question of impairment

Oliver's work is identified by Barnes as underpinned by a materialist analysis. His position on the social model is frequently reproduced and is by now, therefore, familiar to a wide audience. He is also one of the most influential disability theorists in the United Kingdom and because of the clarity of his position, his work is sometimes used as an essential version of the social model, an exemplar for those wishing to debate its adequacy and to question the way that it deals with impairment (Bury 1996; Read 1998). In doing this, it is of course important to recognize the danger of conflating variants of the social model, a process which itself can oversimplify a developing field. Oliver (1996: 33) states the essence of the social model clearly and unequivocally:

> It is not individual limitations of whatever kind, which are the cause of the problem but society's failure to provide appropriate services and adequately ensure the needs of disabled people are fully taken into account in its social organisation.

In Oliver's accounts, disablement is socially created and impairment, of itself, is not seen as being part of the problem. There is no evaluative connotation placed on impairment, which is 'nothing less than a description of the physical body' (Oliver 1996: 35). Hence we see impairments presented as attributes, differences, sets of characteristics among many that human beings may have.

It has sometimes been suggested that the social model in the form outlined by Oliver presents as a somewhat 'oversocialized' or reductionist view of disablement (Bury 1996; Pinder 1996; Williams 1996; Read 1998). It has also been argued that by adopting a rather determinist and extrinsic explanation of human development, behaviour and experience, it does not always give credit to the complexity of the relationships and interactions between individuals and the structures within which they find themselves (Read 1998). In addition, and rather fundamentally, Low (1996) has questioned the validity of the way that disability and discrimination are sometimes defined as indistinguishable, suggesting that this makes the social model true by definition but still begs the question of limitations stemming from bodily disorder or impairment.

More recently, however, it is a number of disabled women writers, informed by feminist politics and scholarship, who have most consistently questioned whether the social model offers a full explanation of the experience of disability (Morris 1991, 1996; French 1993, 1994a; Crow 1996). Of concern to some disabled feminists is the way that the social model neglects the impact of impairment and what Morris terms 'the personal experience of physical or intellectual restriction' (Morris 1991: 10). Within this tradition, Crow (1996) has presented one of the most detailed explorations of the meaning of impairment for individuals, and its relationship with the social model of disability. Discussing disability as a social construct, she suggests:

Sometimes it feels as if this focus is so absolute that we are in danger of assuming that impairment has no part at all in determining our experiences. Instead of tackling the contradictions and complexities of our experience head on, we have chosen in our campaigns to present impairment as irrelevant, neutral and, sometimes positive, but never, ever as the quandary it really is . . .

It is this rejection of impairment that is the social model's flaw. Although social factors *do* generally dominate in determining experience and quality of life . . . impairment *is* relevant. For fear of appearing to endorse mainstream responses, we are in danger of failing to acknowledge that for some individuals impairment – as well as disability – causes disadvantage.

(Crow 1996: 208, 216–17)

From a different perspective, we can find in the work of Abberley (1987, 1996, 1997) an extensive examination of the meaning of impairment and its place within a social theory of disability. He finds it unsurprising that public debate by disabled people on impairment has been limited:

In a world where impaired people are disadvantaged, discriminated against and despised it is to be expected that part of the resistance to this should initially involve a concentration on the unjust social process of disablement, and a corresponding disregard for impairment.

(Abberley 1996: 63)

In his earlier work, Abberley (1987) argues that disabled people, like other groups, are indeed oppressed but that their experience is differentiated by impairment:

In developing theories of sexual and racial oppression it has been necessary for theoreticians of the women's and anti-racist movements to settle accounts with biology, which in both cases have been employed to explain and to justify social disadvantage. For a theory of disability as oppression, however, an important difference arises when we consider the issue of impairment. While in the case of sexual and racial oppression, biological difference serves only as a qualificatory condition of a wholly ideological oppression, for disabled people the biological difference, albeit as I shall argue itself a consequence of social practices, is itself a part of oppression. It is crucial that a theory of disability as oppression comes to grips with this 'real' inferiority, since it forms a bedrock upon which justificatory oppressive theories are based and, psychologically, an immense impediment to the development of political consciousness amongst disabled people. Such a development is systematically blocked through the naturalisation of impairment.

(Abberley 1987: 8)

In the same paper, Abberley emphasizes the social origins of impairment within capitalism and goes on to argue that 'impairment must be identified as a bad thing, insofar as it is an undesirable consequence of a distorted social development, at the same time as it is held to be a positive attribute of the individual who is impaired' (Abberley 1987). He points to the key distinction to be made between the prevention of impairment and the attitudes towards and treatment of people who are already impaired. Disabled modes of living are to be valued but the social production of impairment condemned.

In his more recent work, however, Abberley (1997) argues that it is inconceivable that the ending of capitalism would also see an end to impairment and he also questions whether such a state of affairs would be desirable anyway. He concludes that to serve the interests of disabled people, a theory of disablement must break with models of humanity that are defined by the logic and values of production. It should, he asserts, transcend 'notions of perfectability and production-orientated rationality' (Abberley 1997: 26). He emphasizes the 'authenticity of impaired modes of being' and considers the ideological oppression that arises in relation to those who reject the idea that they or their children should be cured or 'rectified' in some way. He argues for a discussion of the 'ontological status of impairment which is by no means exhausted by simply locating impairment within the individual and disability in society' (Abberley 1996: 65). He concludes, 'As long as there is a general eugenicist consensus between left and right that impaired modes of being are undesirable, disabled people must challenge such views as, in essence, genocidal' (Abberley 1997: 30).

It is small wonder that impairment has proved to be a significant issue theoretically and politically for those disabled writers engaged with the disabled people's movement. As has already been suggested, a great deal of their theoretical work has both grown from and informed the movement and is seen explicitly to be liberational. If for no other reason (and there may be many), this makes any attempt to make a distinction between the theoretical and the political arbitrary and difficult to sustain. When any theoretical work, such as that associated with the social model of disability, is defined as liberational, questioning any of its basic tenets can be viewed as an attack on liberation itself. More specifically, those who explore the potentially restricting nature of impairment or concede any primary role to bodily disorder, may automatically be construed as participating in oppressive ideological practice in relation to themselves or others (French 1993; Williams 1996).

Many acknowledge the political dangers of recognizing any restriction imposed by impairment. There is considerable fear of reconfirming damaging and dominant views which seek to pathologize individual disabled people to the detriment of their human and civil rights (Morris 1991; Crow 1996). There is, however, an equally difficult problem to be faced in maintaining the view of impairment as a neutral attribute, when individuals and groups of disabled people report that they do not experience impairment as neutral or positive at all. On the contrary, some find that it can be a significantly restricting and painful part of their experience as disabled people, though sometimes not in the way supposed by non-disabled people (Booth 1992; Crow 1996).

Any recognition of the restrictive or painful nature of impairment, however, begins to attribute to it meaning and value that is negative and this can cause further (though not necessarily irreconcilable) contradictions in relation to concerted and important efforts to affirm the 'authenticity of impaired modes of being' (Abberley 1996) or the subversion of negative valuations (Shakespeare 1996). The process of subverting negative valuations may not only entail 'becoming what one has learned to despise' (Shakespeare 1996: 106) but may sometimes carry with it the conviction that the only logical corollary is to assert that the prevention of impairment is undesirable or genocidal. The prevention of impairment may be seen to go hand in hand with narrowing of definitions of acceptable ways of being, a process that may be viewed as undermining or dangerous to those disabled people living with impairment. When narrower notions of normality are affirmed or aspired to now or in the future, even more disabled people may find themselves excluded from the definition of what it is to be normal. 'Normal' is not used merely as a descriptive or neutral term. It is not simply about the distribution of characteristics in a given population. It has evaluative aspects and carries with it personal, social and political consequences for those who are seen to fall both within and outside its definitions. In some circumstances, it proves to be only a very short journey from the position of being defined as 'not-normal' to the point of being stripped of rights and aspirations enjoyed by those who remain within the dominant category.

These are very high stakes indeed. Small wonder, then, that some disabled writers have reported pressure to strive towards arbitrary standards of normality (or some approximation of them) even when it runs counter to their interests. By such efforts, have they been taught, they may win approval and 'pass' in a hostile environment (Sutherland 1981; Reisser 1992). Small wonder, too, that some wish to fight tooth and nail uncritical notions of normality and the related denegration of impaired ways of being.

The question of diversity

In resisting narrow definitions of normality and ideologies that they regard as damaging, many activists and writers have come to regard diversity as a central and key concept. As I have already noted, affirming impaired ways of being is seen to be crucial by writers such as Abberley (1987, 1997). Similarly, 'celebrating the difference' and developing pride in positive disabled identities framed by disabled people themselves are important elements in the work of others (e.g. Morris 1991). This may be seen as part of a wider recognition that there is a huge diversity of lifestyles, cultures and experience within the population as a whole. The positive affirmation of diversity has increasingly been argued to be in the interest not only of the different individuals and groups concerned but also of society as a whole. Disabled people may characterize themselves as one group within a highly diverse social structure. As Barnes (1997) points out, however, there has been concern expressed by some that established work on the social model of disablement and other related social theory did not engage, for example, with issues of ethnicity and gender. In other words, the question of diversity among disabled people themselves initially received less attention than some would have wished.

More recently, there has been growing recognition of the notion that while there undoubtedly exists a commonality of position and experience among disabled people, social divisions within the disabled people's movement and within the population as a whole are of enormous significance. It has been increasingly acknowledged that the differential experience of individuals and groups that is related to their social class, minority ethnic status, gender, age and sexuality should be recognized and accorded a primacy that has sometimes been ignored. Of course it is by no means unusual in any social movement and related academic discourse, for diversity of view and difference in experience to go on the back burner in favour of reclaimed identity and common cause. Almost inevitably at some point, however, the question is raised about whether the unified accounts truly reflect the variety of significant and formative experience of all participants in the movement. It has been argued by some that it can no longer be assumed that for any individual, disability is the sole or significant identity (Shakespeare 1996).

The 1990s have seen, therefore, an expansion in debate, research and writing which focuses on the way that the experience of disability intersects with the experience of membership of other social divisions (e.g. Baxter *et al.* 1990; Begum 1992; Stuart 1993; Begum *et al.* 1994; Corbett 1994; Keith 1994; Morris 1996; Shakespeare *et al.* 1996). There is exploration of the ways in which the experience of Black disabled people is different in some of its aspects from that of their white peers and of the distinctive nature of the oppression and discrimination that they encounter. Disabled feminists have given substantial attention to the respects in which their experience as disabled women reflects the gendered nature of wider social relations. They have also utilized feminist scholarship and the history and politics of the women's movement to inform disability politics and theory.

There is inevitably disagreement and debate both within the disabled people's movement and outside it about some key aspects of a developing social theory of disablement, including ways of understanding individual impairment, diversity and difference and the implications of this for disabled people's rights. This does not preclude, however, broad theoretical and political agreement among many that some of the most oppressive, if not *the* most oppressive features of disabled people's lives are socially and politically constructed and can be challenged or ameliorated by social and political means. Across a spectrum of opinion in the past 10 years, there has been an increasing consensus on the need to challenge the social exclusion, devaluation and dehumanization routinely experienced by disabled children and adults.

Dehumanization, devaluation and exclusion

Central to the work of many is the notion that dominant ideology devalues disabled people and their lives and defines them as exceptions to commonly-held notions of people and citizens (e.g. Abberley 1987; Morris 1991). In the early 1980s, the mother of a young son with learning disabilities deliberated on his position as an outsider in a world seen primarily to belong to others:

> People think of our children as something separate – when they think of them at all. They're not even in the same category as those who've had a dramatic accident and become paralysed . . . because you see, they were once 'real' people, and that's what makes the difference. If you were never 'real' then you're best left forgotten.
>
> (Read 1985: 118)

The kernel of her observation is that disabled children explicitly or by implication have been argued out of the category of what it is to be 'real', to be human, and therefore, to have the rights and values attributed to those with such status. She suggests that the only reason why some disabled children may be seen differently from her son is because once at least, they had that status and lost it. The ways in which the discrimination against disabled children and adults has been reinforced and legitimated through their dehumanization by others is a recurring and developing theme in the literature of the past two decades. Abberley (1987: 16) describes the way that 'oppressive theories of disability systematically distort and stereotype the identities of their putative subjects, restricting their full humanity by constituting them only in their "problem" aspects.'

Increasingly, writers and activists have been documenting and drawing attention to the ways in which disabled people have consistently been construed as marginal to the dominant social order. Pervasive ideology and discourse, often in the most commonplace and familiar forms, make it possible and legitimate for disabled children and adults to endure experiences and conditions which would not be regarded as acceptable for their non-disabled peers.

There is, however, one issue above all others that makes the fragility of the position of disabled people crystal clear. As Shearer (1984) points out, it gets to the very heart of the way our society views disabled people, particularly when they have considerable impairments. I refer here to the recurring public debates on whether some have the right to life at all. This is not an issue that can be confined to the history of the Holocaust (Morris 1991) or the eugenics movement (Ryan and Thomas 1980; Read 1987) for it has come to the fore time and time again during the past two decades. Public debates have frequently been linked to legal disputes in Great Britain and in the United States which have centred on whether there are circumstances that permit parents and medical personnel to take the decision that a young disabled child, often a baby, should not survive (Shearer 1984).

For example, within the lifetime of the sons and daughters of the West Midlands mothers, the trial of Leonard Arthur in 1980 and 1981 provided a context where dominant assumptions about disabled people (which often remain inexplicit) were openly articulated with starkness and clarity. Leonard Arthur, a paediatrician, was found not guilty of the attempted murder of John Pearson, a baby with Down's syndrome whose parents did not wish him to survive. This was not a situation where the decisions and ensuing debates are complicated by life having only been saved or sustained through advanced technological intervention. In this case, it was argued powerfully and publicly by many that giving a baby sedation and nursing care only – a process that inevitably results in death – was justified if the child is rejected by his parents and if he is also 'irreversibly disabled'. In court and elsewhere, arguments that would not have been countenanced for a non-disabled child, were seen as perfectly admissable simply because the baby had Down's syndrome (Shearer 1984; Read 1987). It was not only that this baby and others like him were characterized as having lives that were not worth living. Shearer (1984) also describes how one professional journal welcomed the acquittal and affirmed the action taken by the paediatrician on financial grounds, arguing that the cost of preserving the life of one subnormal [*sic*] baby meant depriving other people of procedures such as hip-replacements and the chance to return to a useful, pain-free life. By such logic John Pearson, simply by his survival alone, would have been held personally and directly responsible for depriving others of beneficial medical interventions. He is placed in the category of the useless and burdensome who not only take their toll on resources but also impede the useful and the productive. Public opinion polling undertaken at the time also revealed overwhelming support for the notion that provided there was parental consent, it should not be seen as murder when medical staff brought about the death of disabled babies (Shearer 1984).

A different but related example is provided by the experience of a mother who disagreed strongly with what she found was accepted and common practice when her daughter was born. In the 1980s, the drawing up of criteria for a predicted quality of life was a common procedure in relation to some groups of disabled children. Frequently, for example, decisions about whether to proceed with or withhold life-saving interventions for children with spina bifida were based on such predictions. The mother wrote about how her daughter, by then a 5-year-old schoolgirl, had survived despite everything:

> Our daughter, Sophie, has spina bifida and hydrocephalus. When she was born she was assessed by a paediatrician and was found to fulfil several of the criteria on a list drawn up by Professor Lorber, a leading light in the treatment of spina bifida in Sheffield. Sophie had hydrocephalus before she was born, her lesion was in an unfavourable position in the lumbar region of her spine, leaving her with some hip and knee flexion. We were told that Sophie wouldn't walk, that she would be brain-damaged and that she would be doubly incontinent. It was suggested that Sophie's quality of life would be so poor that she should not be treated and allowed to die.
>
> When it was clear that Sophie had every intention to live and thrive she had a valve and shunt system inserted into her brain, draining into her stomach, and she was reassessed.
>
> (Tippett 1990: 19)

Similarly, there has been not inconsiderable concern and some demands for redress over the alleged unwillingness on the part of some medical staff, until recent years, to undertake heart surgery on children with Down's syndrome, even when the predicted outcomes were held to be good (BBC 1998). Non-intervention could result in a more restricted life, pain and discomfort and premature death.

It is not my intention here to underestimate the complexity of some decisions that have to be made, particularly in view of recent advances in technology and the unprecedented possibilities this opens up for saving and sustaining life. Some situations have to be faced that simply did not occur in the past. In addition, it should be recognized that public debates on these questions have not remained static since the 1980s. Among other things, there are indications that in recent times, local authorities have been more active in seeking to ensure that the rights of disabled children in such difficult circumstances have a greater degree of protection than in the past.

This does not, however, change the underlying point being made. With or without the complicating factors of advanced medical technology, debates about whether disabled children should survive or should be entitled to medical interventions, tend inevitably to reveal commonplace and damaging attitudes held by many about disabled children and adults more generally. Aside from concerns about the legal and human rights of the individuals involved in any particular case, these debates and the assumptions that are frequently expressed, provide an unimaginably hostile context for other disabled children and adults and those close to them. They may be presented time and time again and in a myriad of ways with a dominant perception that they neither have nor lead lives worth living, experiences in themselves exceptionally eroding of self-worth. Added to this, it would not be surprising were some to have the uneasy feeling that had they been judged disabled enough and been reached early enough, they would not have survived at all. It is difficult to imagine a more fragile place to be than one where you have a sense that others might see it as perfectly legitimate to kill you for what you *are* rather than because of anything that you may have done.

While assumptions underpinning debates about the legitimacy of bringing about the deaths of disabled children or withholding medical treatment provide stark and concentrated indications of the oppression of disabled people, the devaluation and discrimination that they face takes more everyday and familiar forms. The routine nature of the personal devaluation and exclusion has been documented, as have the commonplace misunderstandings about their lives and needs that are held by non-disabled people (Morris 1991, 1996). One problem about such misunderstandings is that because non-disabled people are generally to be found formally and informally in stronger positions of power than their disabled peers, they are often well-placed to impose their views and make them stick.

In formal and informal ways, in ideological discourse and in institutionalized practices, disabled people find themselves systematically excluded not only from everyday events, experiences and locations but also, insidiously, from dominant definitions of significant social groupings. Definitions of society and groups within it are often used in ways that are not inclusive of disabled people who are frequently framed by others as a discrete and exceptional grouping without right of inclusion in other social divisions to which they might legitimately claim membership (e.g Morris 1993b). For example, terms such as 'society', 'men', 'women', 'Black people', 'Black women', 'gay men' and so on, have often been used to lay claim to the *whole* defining category when in reality, they refer most often only to those who are most dominant within it. Frequently that does not mean disabled people.

The sites on which the devaluation and exclusion take place are innumerable and omnipresent and discourses that either leave them out or explicitly frame them as outsiders are pervasive. These practices and ideologies are built into the bricks and mortar of our formal institutions and they seep into our personal encounters and observations. Disabled people are absent from places where they would wish to be and present in locations that confirm their disadvantage and subordination. When they appear, they are often characterized in ways not in their interests.

One of the most comprehensive surveys of these sites of discrimination and oppression was conducted by Barnes (1991). He argues the case for anti-discrimination legislation by documenting the consistent disadvantage and discrimination experienced by disabled people in key areas such as education, employment, income maintenance, health and social care, housing and daily living, transport, the built environment, social life, leisure facilities, the media, and politics. Others have concentrated on the discriminatory attitudes to disabled people's sexuality and parenthood (Finger 1991; Shakespeare *et al.* 1996), on the oppressive responses to which they are subjected in public places (Keith 1996) and on the distorted images of them that are often projected by charities and the media (Hannaford 1985; Morris 1991; Hevey 1992).

When these sites of oppression are considered, it is clearly not realistic to see them as separate or discrete areas, for in many cases, the disadvantage experienced in one area will have a knock-on effect in others. This widespread and interlocking nature of different disadvantaging experiences makes it difficult to focus exclusively on any one site of discrimination without oversimplifying significant features of the context and processes involved. Employment, however, may provide one useful and important illustration of the ways in which a range of experiences conspire to leave a disabled person substantially disadvantaged.

Research conducted over the past two decades has consistently indicated that economically active disabled people face greater barriers than their non-disabled peers in relation to job opportunities, a disadvantaged position that cannot be explained wholly by their functional abilities (Walker 1982; Lonsdale 1990; Barnes 1991; Anderson 1995; Thornton *et al.* 1997). As a group, they are more likely to face unemployment and to be among the long-term unemployed. When in work, they are more frequently in lower paid, lower status jobs. There is also evidence of the way that discrimination, ignorance and an unwillingness to make minor and reasonable adjustments to the environment of the workplace and working practices affect their chances. There are indications that some employers act on untested stereotypical assumptions about people's working potential and that some also react negatively to difference in appearance. Disabled people have often had a more restricted education and been offered fewer training opportunities (Walker 1982; Lonsdale 1990; Gooding 1994; NACAB 1994; Anderson 1995).

In addition to problems in relation to the workplace, education and training, disabled people's already limited opportunities may be further exacerbated by factors such as a lack of adequate transport provision designed to accommodate their needs. It may simply prove to be a problem for a disabled person to get to a place of work without undue difficulty and fatigue (Gooding 1994).

For those without jobs, there are personal and financial consequences. Rightly or wrongly, people are often accorded and in turn themselves derive value and esteem from being in paid work. The workplace provides a location for making social contacts, and the working day and the working week give some structure and routine. Finding an alternative route to using time purposefully and feeling good about that and about yourself is not always easy. In addition, disabled people without jobs face the associated economic disadvantage (Bertoud *et al.* 1993). The lack of income combined with bearing the extra costs of disabled living, means having a more restricted access to goods and services that are a taken-for-granted part of the lifestyles of many who are earning (Read 1987; Barnes 1991). Without strong measures to counter such interrelated restrictions, the circle appears very tightly closed.

The oppressive dimensions of service provision

Another consistently emerging theme in recent literature is that services that are widely assumed to be relief-giving, supportive and enabling to disabled children and adults, may in part at least, reproduce the damaging ideologies that have been discussed and the practices stemming from them (Read 1991; French 1994b). This is not to say, of course, that all service provision is of this nature and that there are not practitioners who have helped to break new ground in the interests of disabled children and adults. Nevertheless over the past 20 years it has increasingly been argued that those services and institutions that are supposed to intervene to improve things may themselves be part of the problem. They too play a part in keeping disabled children and adults in their marginalized position, restricting their autonomy and limiting their choices. For some, they provide the site of extremely damaging and unhappy experiences.

The process has been documented whereby historically disabled children and adults have consistently been segregated into separate educational, health and social care institutions, a practice which to some degree persists today. There have been a growing number of accounts of the lives that they have led (e.g.Oswin 1978, 1984, 1998; Ryan and Thomas 1980; Sutherland

1981; Tomlinson 1982; Hannaford 1985; Barton 1986; Humphries and Gordon 1992; Smith 1994; Morris 1995, 1998; French 1996; Kennedy 1996; Smith 1998). Many of these accounts do not make happy reading. This is not to suggest that a boarding school, for example, never was or is the right choice for a disabled (or non-disabled) child. Nor is it to suggest that communal living for children and adults is always bad. What is being noted here is the development of systems that are founded on the assumption that disabled children and adults should automatically be segregated, and prescribes for them a markedly different life experience from that of their non-disabled peers.

Apart from the deprivation of opportunities that, in decent circumstances, may be gained from living in the outside world and a dislocation from formative and sustaining experiences that others regard as ordinary, it is clear that institutional life has frequently fallen far short of anything that a child or adult could rightly be expected to endure. Sometimes they have been given something that is of quality in one area but restrictive and damaging in another; sometimes the controlling and rigid nature of an institution has produced excessive regimentation and restriction of the individuals who lived there; sometimes what was offered was simply unimaginative, careless, narrow or ill-informed; sometimes the environment was so low in expectations that children's and adults' abilities and potential for acting on the world were dampened or irradicated; sometimes their lives were bleak and joyless; sometimes they were subjected to routine abuse either because of the inclinations and power of individual workers or because of practices endemic and accepted in a particular institution or system. For many children and adults, these were not brief experiences. They were confined for long periods, sometimes a lifetime, with no choice or control over their lives, no possibility of progress and no redress for wrongs inflicted upon them.

Some services other than the total or segregated institution have also been criticized by disabled and non-disabled writers for the part that they play in reproducing inequality and maintaining injustice. There is considerable unease and anger about the way that many services are seen to exercise control over disabled people and maintain them in a dependent situation, prescribing what they should have and how they should live. Care, it is suggested, is frequently control by another name (Morris 1993a). There is also some dissatisfaction with therapeutic and rehabilitative services that adhere to uncritical notions of normalization or that concentrate solely on encouraging change or adaptation by the disabled person, even when their capacity to achieve this is limited and the environment to which they are expected to adapt is hostile to their needs (Oliver 1990; French 1994a, 1994b). Relatedly, there has been concern about those professionals whose philosophy and practice implies that disabled people can only have autonomy and choice in their lives through the achievement of functional independence and who ignore alternative approaches and services that can enhance choice and quality of life (Oliver 1990; Read 1998). It has been argued that there is a need to challenge professional practice, which gives a message to disabled people that they are valued only if they strive to become someone and something that they are not and could never be (Read 1998). The negative and undermining effects both of being recipients of charity and of being presented as such, have been described consistently (Hannaford 1985; Morris 1991; Hevey 1992).

In common with many others, disabled people have discovered the contradictory nature of the experience of being users of state and voluntary sector services. They have found that there is a price to be paid and that invaluable assistance frequently comes conjoined with oppression (Gliedman and Roth 1980). When they are being 'done good to', they may find that they are really being put in their place.

Disabled people gaining ground

There is clearly a very great deal in the literature produced by disabled people and others which supports and reflects the concerns of the West Midlands mothers. There is undoubtedly much about the way the world operates that runs counter to the interests of disabled children and adults. The widespread nature of the barriers that they face must at times make change seem unlikely or overwhelmingly difficult. Some of the West Midlands mothers felt, however, that while things could be very bad indeed, some change for the better had taken place. They had witnessed more open and positive discussion about disability in the media and elsewhere, and some improvement in conditions and attitudes generally. More disabled children and adults formed a visible presence in public places. Some service provision was enabling and supportive. It was no longer necessary to fight quite so hard to secure a mainstream school place for a disabled child, and so on.

There is certainly a sense more generally that some ground has been won and that the rights of disabled people as citizens are now more firmly on the policy agenda in a number of ways. Increasingly, official reports and policy documents reflect, in part at least, the position that has been argued forcefully by the disabled people's movement and its associates (e.g. Stevens 1991).

As far as some disabled people are concerned, some changes characterized by others as gains may seem to be too little too late or at best, of dubious value. The Disability Discrimination Act 1995, the first piece of legislation to counter discrimination against disabled people in Britain, provides one such example. It was introduced only reluctantly, and because of what were seen to be its limited powers, widely condemned by many disabled individuals and organizations representing the interests of disabled people (Gooding 1994). While recognizing its severe limitations, others have seen it as a small milestone, a first statement of its kind and a tool that may be possible to use to the advantage of disabled people.

The 1990s have also seen a substantial policy shift towards recharacterizing clients of state, voluntary and private health and social care services as consumers who should be afforded choice (Griffiths 1988). In this context, many have argued strongly for legislation and provision which increase the autonomy of disabled people to choose what they would find acceptable and useful without dependence on professional goodwill and mediation (Morris 1993a). The second half of the 1990s has seen the introduction of a number of measures which allow this to become a reality for some disabled people at least. The Community Care (Direct Payments) Act 1996 provides one such example. This legislation allows local authorities to give financial aid to service users to enable them to purchase assistance and other services directly themselves.

Concluding comments

There is a great deal to be found in research and other literature which reflects the view held by the West Midlands mothers that the organization of contemporary society frequently runs counter to the interests of their sons and daughters. There is much in the rapidly expanding field of disability studies which supports their sense that the world and many of the people in it misunderstand their children and close down spaces that they could rightly occupy and opportunities that they could reasonably have. There can also be found a great deal of evidence to justify their view that the erosion of their sons' and daughters' well-being and sense of self-worth is an ever-present danger which calls for vigilance.

Bearing all of this in mind, it is clearly crucial not to underestimate the extent of change that would need to occur before disabled people could routinely expect to have human and civil rights anywhere near on a par with their non-disabled peers. It is equally important, however, to recognize the evidence of things being on the move in the past decade or so. The West Midlands mothers themselves acknowledged the changes that they had witnessed across their sons' and daughters' childhoods. They felt that there was still a long way to go but that some significant progress had been achieved. Some disabled writers, too, have focused upon the gains that have been made, particularly as a result of collective action by the Disabled People's Movement. It is perhaps most appropriate, therefore, to finish this section of the book with the reflections of one of the most influential activists of recent times. Morris (1991: 4) describes the sense of things changing as she gives an account of a conversation that she had with a friend after she became disabled in the 1980s:

> And I remember Jane saying that if ever there was a time in history when it was exciting to be disabled it must be now, when disabled people were starting to organise, challenge the prejudice they experienced and demand their right to a decent quality of life.

 **6**

Mediators and allies on the ground

In this final chapter, I want to draw together a number of themes from the rest of the book and link them with the experience of motherhood and mothering in relation to disabled children and young people. I particularly want to consider the women's role as mediators in their sons' and daughters' lives. I shall suggest that the active mediation that they undertake comes about because the women witness what they perceive to be unacceptable, exclusionary or devaluing responses to their children. Their role as mediators carries with it substantial hazards and dilemmas as well as considerable positive outcomes.

I would argue that in many respects, the ways that mothers of disabled children have been characterized over time can be understood as distilled and magnified versions of accounts of motherhood more generally. Just as these understandings have not always served all women well, when applied to mothers of disabled children, they have sometimes given rise to particularly unappreciative or partial interpretations of their lives.

I also want to suggest that there is another story to be told. When we consider the perspectives of mothers of disabled children themselves, what research tells us about the lives they lead and insights that can be gained from the literature on disability and oppression, a different version can emerge. We can begin to appreciate why certain interlocking conditions are likely to give rise to particular understandings of their children and the world in which they live as well as characteristic mothering practices, including mediation. When we ground the mothers' perspectives in both their immediate and broader social contexts, we may develop a greater degree of understanding about some activities that they undertake and approaches that they adopt.

In an earlier part of the book, I also suggested that when we look at motherhood on the margins, we learn a great deal about motherhood more generally and the limitations of some dominant accounts of it. Mothers of disabled children may be considered to be just such mothers on the margins. While we are focusing in the main on their distinctive experience, we also need to recognize that in doing so, we can infer much about the way that all mothering is grounded in the social and material circumstances in which it takes place. While it is important to acknowledge the singular features of the experience of mothers of disabled children, it is also important to be aware of the danger of ascribing to them a marginalized or exotic status that ghettoizes them still further, divides them from other mothers and strips their lives of the ordinary qualities and aspirations that they may value.

Mother blaming

Earlier in this book, I drew attention to work which argued strongly that the rules of good mothering and the ideals of good motherhood have increasingly come under the scrutiny of experts and that the demands placed on mothers have been expanded and extended in scope (Smart 1996). As we explore the experience of mothers of disabled children and the interpretations placed upon it, it is crucial to acknowledge the extent to which they find themselves under the microscope. As is clear from the accounts of the West Midlands mothers and from a wide range of research, being the mother of a disabled child entails contact with substantial numbers of professionals and involvement in many types of assessment. In their role as mothers, the women appear in front of paid experts far more often than most and in these circumstances, their mothering and other people's perceptions of it become much more public. Aspects of their lives which many regard as private become shared property, open to the speculations of others who are mostly in a stronger position of power. A child's upbringing may become professionalized, with mothers under considerable pressure to do the 'right' thing in the 'right' way according to the professional edicts of the time. Sometimes that can run counter to a mother's sense of what constitutes a good upbringing overall for her child (Gregory 1991).

It is not only that professionals are able to frame what good mothering should consist of and make demands on women accordingly, but it needs also to be borne in mind that should they think fit, paid experts are in a position to change their minds quite fundamentally within a relatively short period. Consequently, they may make contradictory appraisals of and demands on mothers within the lifespan of one disabled child. For example, the mother of a child with physical impairments who wanted mainstream education in the early 1980s was not unlikely to face professionals who saw her as unrealistic, possibly irresponsible and as not having come to terms with her child's limitations. The same mother today has at least a sporting chance of being thought of as trying to offer her child something which conforms to agreed best practice in many areas of the country. The mother of a son now 20 years old, who pressed for his inclusion in mainstream school at a time when it was unfashionable, may now feel vindicated and pleased that things have changed. She may also remember, however, the personal cost and the hurt she experienced at the way her motivation and aspirations for him were scrutinized at an earlier time.

In previous chapters, I drew on work that suggested that all mothers' responsibilities and proximity to their children have tended to make them prime suspects when things are seen to go wrong in their children's lives. The mother's activities are not always understood in context and many other influences on the child and the household which affect what can be achieved are often ignored. Explanations of problems which children encounter tend to be predominantly individualistic. Good mothering is seen to be a highly significant, if not *the* significant factor and is often characterized solely in terms of a set of personal attributes fixed to the mother herself.

I also referred earlier to ubiquitous mother paradigms with which we all become familiar: stereotypes such as the all-sacrificing angel and the overindulgent mother who is really satisfying her own needs at the expense of her children's independence. While such representations of mothers and motherhood are potentially hazardous for all women with children, they may be especially so for the mother of the disabled child. As we have seen, whatever she or her child would otherwise choose given different circumstances, the demands placed upon the mother–child relationship often go far beyond what is expected of those between non-disabled children and their mothers. The mother is required to be present much more and to do much more. There is no escaping the fact that she becomes a key figure. She is frequently by her child's side at times when other children would not be with their mothers. The child often relies upon her in ways that other children do not and for longer periods across their lifespan. If we analyse this relationship predominantly in terms of the personal attributes and inclinations of those individuals involved, rather than understanding it in part at least as the outcome of specific social processes, the stage is set for casting the mother in the role of self-sacrificing angel, overpossessive demon or other, milder variants on the same themes.

Mary, one of the West Midlands women, described her discomfort at the way people sometimes cast her in the former role. She took offence both because it did not represent how she felt about herself and because it spoke volumes about what those people thought of her son. For mothers in Mary's position, however, there is the ever-present danger of being transformed from the all-sacrificing angel to the overpossessive demon. The two are surprisingly close and present something of a knife edge for the women concerned. It is only a short journey from being in the role of the one who is wonderful because she copes with everything in a way that astounds others, to the point of being reallocated the part of the overpowering mother who does too much and will not let go. The former can be admired, though preferably from a distance, while the latter is the target of much criticism.

I have also argued that a number of established theoretical frameworks, and the ways that they were used, opened up and maintained the possibilities for undue mother-blaming. We have seen the central role accorded to the early mother–child relationship within psychoanalytic literature and the consequences that there were seen to be for the child when that relationship did not develop in the prescribed form. We have also seen the influence of psychoanalytic theory both generally and on the approaches taken to understanding families who had disabled children. At one stage in the post-Second World War period, professional literature on disabled children and those close to them focused almost entirely on intrapsychic and intrafamilial issues to the neglect of other influences. The interpretation of parents' reactions and behaviours and the offering of psychotherapeutic intervention could form a major part of the small amount of professional practice that was on offer. Parents, particularly mothers, were susceptible to being pathologized in a number of ways, while significant needs and circumstances in their lives remained unacknowledged or neglected.

I have also argued that while mothers may sometimes have been held to account for *not* mothering in the prescribed way, at other times they have been blamed for allegedly doing precisely that. Those who have wished to challenge and change what they regard as a dominant and damaging social order have often regarded socialization by mothers as the very thing that works powerfully to maintain it. The mother is seen as one of the main actors responsible for teaching children, adults-in-the-making, their ascribed place within society. She is construed as one of the main conduits through which dominant discourse flows.

If we apply such a view of the world, or elements of it, to the situation of mothers and their disabled sons and daughters, we can see how the women might easily be characterized as some of the main barriers to their children's having access to new opportunities for self-realization. As awareness is growing about disabled children's and adults' rights as citizens, and as disabled people increasingly challenge the established social order, it is now more common for activists and practitioners to consider the social processes that impede access to experiences that others take for granted. There is a danger that those whose view of mothering is the top-down and uncritical transmission of dominant and established values may stereotype mothers of disabled children as some of the most conservative forces in their sons' and daughters' lives. The mother may too easily be caricatured as someone who has not yet attained enlightenment, who stands in the way of progress and who accepts and reinforces without question more established ways of thinking. She may find herself as susceptible as ever to a dose of good, old-fashioned mother-blaming.

Mothers as allies on the ground

In Chapter 3, I also considered more recent work on mothering and motherhood that sees the women concerned as active subjects who are involved in rational, interpretive processes (e.g. Graham 1993b; Everingham 1994; Mayall 1996). They are not portrayed as women who passively absorb preordained social norms and socialize their children accordingly. Rather, they are seen as sifting and sorting raw information in an effort to come to decisions about what they think is best for their children. While their capacity to make judgements and to act is significant, their actions and attributes need not be viewed in an individualistic or purely personalized way. There is recognition of both the limitations and the opportunities afforded by the social structures and processes that impact upon them and their children. Their work as mothers entails their making sensitive, context-dependent judgements and decisions on a day-to-day basis. They have to decide what can be achieved in the circumstances and frame a strategy accordingly.

Such approaches to motherhood and mothering tend to be more appreciative of the women's perspectives and seek to understand their actions in relation to the social context in which they occur. These decisions and practices have a rationale that can be more readily understood when the women's accounts are heard. To hear women's contextualized interpretations and explanations and to be appreciative of them does not necessitate idealizing nor even agreeing with them in every respect. However, when we are given an explanation of *what* women are trying to do and *why* they are trying to do it in relation to the context in which the decision is made, we have still been offered access to a very great deal that enhances our understanding.

One of the most interesting features of some recent work on motherhood (e.g. Mayall 1996) is that while it emphasizes the fact that women make context-dependent decisions, it does not reduce these to the status of unthinking pragmatism. On the contrary, the strength and integrity of the decisions is, in part, seen to grow from the very fact that they are grounded in and responsive to the complexities of the context. A significant element of that context can be seen to be the mother–child relationship itself. Mothers come to agreements and decisions that are underpinned by moral values which they have developed partly as a result of their involvement in a committed and intimate relationship.

This is not to present an idealized version of the way that mother–child relationships work. Mothers may be motivated in part by ethical notions of what *could* and *should* be, but they are also only human, and therefore susceptible to a range of influences, including battle fatigue. When we reflect on the taxing and ongoing demands made on many mothers, including those with disabled children, it would be very surprising indeed were they not to take the pragmatic short-cut sometimes for the sake of day-to-day survival. We know that difficult circumstances and life events leave some mothers with little surplus energy once the bare survival tasks are accomplished. It would be extraordinary if some women did not withdraw from the fray from time to time, offer less than they would otherwise wish, the better to fight another day.

An approach such as this can be very illuminating of the strategies adopted by many mothers of disabled children. The way that it describes the process of mothering is often redolent of the accounts given by mothers themselves, including the West Midlands women. They and their children are thrown together in close relationships that are constructed and reconstructed over time through the care of the child's or young person's emotional and bodily well-being, the more so because there may not be the opportunity for the child's needs to be met effectively by others. This particular type of intimacy and involvement may well exceed that which occurs between mothers and their non-disabled children. The relationship, however protracted, is defined by and grounded in parent–child love and in many cases may be energized by it.

Sometimes the child's care is provided directly by the mother and sometimes it is arranged by her but in any event, she is likely to be closely involved. The intimate mother–child relationship is both a central force and context for generating and determining decisions about what might be in the child's interests as well as the best means to achieve it in the given circumstances. Close and fine-grained observation and interaction give rise both to judgements about what outcomes are desirable and to practical strategies for achieving them.

It would be simplistic to view this mothering either as an exclusively top-down or bottom-up activity. Mayall (1996) proposes a more interactive view. She suggests that while children's needs and wants structure the relationship, it is also something of a collaborative enterprise with mother and child finding the best workable balance that can be achieved in the circumstances. Given the lack of support available to many households with disabled children, the needs of the disabled child may be particularly powerful in structuring the relationship directly and indirectly. There is also evidence, however, that mothers put their own stamp on the proceedings by developing their own characteristic coping strategies to maintain a workable equilibrium (Beresford 1994). The West Midlands women provided copious examples of the varied and personalized ways that they approached managing situations where there were actual or potential conflicts of interest. They were intent on meeting the disabled child's needs while taking other factors in the situation into account. Angela spoke repeatedly of 'balancing everything out'.

Creating a balance that is workable for both mother and child, as well as reaching conclusions about essential needs to be met, is much more taxing in some circumstances than others. As we have seen, studies repeatedly demonstrate how poverty, ethnic status and lone parenthood are powerful mediating factors that determine the room for manoeuvre that children and their mothers have and the choices that they can make. In conditions of material hardship and social exclusion, mothers and children frequently go without or mothers meet the child's needs at their own expense. In these exacting circumstances, the women have to be very resourceful and fight very hard indeed in order to create the space for their child to flourish (Graham 1993b).

A number of writers have proposed that it is helpful to see mothers of both disabled and non-disabled children as their children's allies on the ground (Read 1991; Mayall 1996; Murray and Penman 1996). While there is no wish to deny the potential conflicts of interest and view between children and their mothers, it is also acknowledged that when it comes to children's welfare, common cause often exists between them. As the mothers develop judgements about what they feel would be good for their children, they come across barriers that stand in the way of their child's needs being met. They then put themselves out to challenge those things that they regard as harsh and contrary to their children's interests. The ally mediates to strike a new balance, negotiating to win a better deal for a child. This sometimes entails swimming against the prevailing tide and challenging the dominant social order.

This view of mothering stands in sharp contrast to one that construes the activity as being exclusively to do with the uncritical socialization of a child according to established and dominant ideology. In this version, the mother is much more active in resisting things that she regards as running counter to her child's well-being. She may not always be successful in her challenges but as mediator and ally, she nevertheless conducts a substantial amount of guerrilla warfare on the child's behalf. She looks for the room for manoeuvre that they both have, and finds out what gains can be made within it. Sometimes mothers come to the conclusion that they cannot change features of the immediate or wider context that work against their children. This may be because they feel the forces ranged against them are too large, that they themselves are unequal to the task for other reasons, that there are insufficient practical resources to make something really work for the child despite what they might want in an ideal world and so on. As an alternative in these circumstances, many try to help their children to develop resilience and coping strategies without condoning the things that they regard as wrong.

It can be argued that the power relations between mother and child are unequal and that it may be mostly in the hands of the mother to decide what is in the interests of her child and what can realistically be achieved. This may be particularly the case when a child's or young person's ability and opportunity to communicate with and through others is limited. Such young people may be reliant both upon their mothers' interpretations of their needs and their willingness to follow them through. The moral imperative that grows from an attentive relationship, however, may provide some safeguards against the abuse of power or against the child's wishes and preferences being entirely lost. For any of us, the wish and intention to do well by someone for whom we feel love and commitment gives no guarantee of getting everything right, but it may provide not a bad baseline from which to start.

As we saw from the accounts of the West Midlands mothers, like all relationships, alliances can be uneven and can vary in strength and reliability from time to time. At some points, the shared understanding of what needs to be done may be strong and enduring. At other times, mothers and children may come to a tacit or explicit agreement on those things on which they can proceed together and those that are no-go areas. Mothers and their sons and daughters may fall out for a while and then regroup over a specific and agreed common cause. Sometimes when the relationship becomes strained, the good ally has no choice but to ride out the storm in the best way she can while keeping doors open.

Some might query whether the degree of direct involvement that mothers continue to have with their disabled sons and daughters is advisable and also whether mothers are appropriate allies and mediators. The problem is that at present, even when it might be desirable, few disabled children are offered high quality services that are an acceptable alternative to the direct care and assistance provided by their mothers. A similar situation applies in relation to advocacy and mediation. If the mothers do not do it, there are currently few who can and will stand in their stead and meet the disabled child's or young person's needs in this respect in a reliable, detailed and consistent way. This is particularly evident when we consider the range of mediation that appears to be needed for many children and young people whose needs may be quite complex. If an ally is to be effective, the commitment, knowledge and time that is required is considerable. Being in the domestic and private sphere, much of the detail of the mother's deliberation, knowledge and skill is hidden from view. It can be all too easy to underestimate the fragments of formal and informal information that she records on the tally, the complexity of the con- text-based decisions that she makes and the juggling she does in order to strike an achievable balance.

If we take only one example, that of mediation in relation to service pro- vision addressed in earlier chapters, some of the problems become apparent. It is clear that good services which meet need are often thin on the ground and delivered through arrangements that are unfamiliar and unfathomable to many people. We have also considered the oppressive dimensions of some ser- vices as well as the limited opportunities that they offer to disabled children and adults. Despite progress being made, high quality services are simply not read- ily available for all who need and might benefit from them. Without an advo- cate or ally, it can be very difficult indeed for many disabled children or adults to make even limited headway on quite basic matters. There have been advances in advocacy and self-advocacy practice in relation to young people who are disabled and in some circumstances this can offer a positive alternative to representation of their interests by mothers and other family members. It is still, however, a relatively underdeveloped provision and it is clear that there are not currently legions of advocates or indeed key workers and care managers who can develop an ongoing, informed and enabling relationship with the majority of children and young people who might benefit from it. In their absence, then, it often falls just as it has always fallen, to the mother to be the best ally that she can be in relation to this one area of mediation among many.

As a mediator and advocate, the woman bases her decisions and her plans of action on the information and judgements that she can muster and on her commitment to her son's or daughter's perceived well-being. The process of becoming mediators and allies on the ground does not happen overnight. It is something that mothers often take on incrementally as experience dictates that it is necessary. Few mothers may start out by anticipating becoming their disabled child's ally or advocate over a protracted period. As the literature on informal caring indicates, the relationship is derived from commitments built up over years and determined by a mixture of 'love, duty, affection and obli- gation' (Finch 1989: 242). The women concerned take on the job because it needs to be done and someone has to do it. They are there, they are most involved and they often have the most detailed knowledge about their child. The job of mediator and ally becomes an almost inevitable extension of their role as mothers who love their children. As they modify and augment their views about their children, their children's place in the world and the need to safeguard their interests, they find themselves increasingly and irrevocably drawn into the role of go-between and the buffer state. Many do not take to the role easily but feel that they have no alternative. It is not uncommon for women to reflect on the significant personal change that they undergo as a result of having to take on this challenging work (Read 1985).

In the remaining sections of the chapter, I want to consider in more detail why mothers become and continue to be mediators for their disabled children and to explore some features of the experience which appear to be significant to them.

Moving to the other side of the track

Not all women, on finding that they have a disabled child, feel the initial shock and unhappiness that has been reported by many (Glendinning 1983). One obvious mediating factor is how the mother and those around her view disability generally and what has been their previous personal experience of it. We saw in an earlier chapter how, as a disabled woman herself, Mason (1992) described the birth of her disabled baby in very positive terms. As Ann, one of the West Midlands mothers found, the presence of another disabled parent can sometimes shape ideas and give untold support. Even those who have a close personal experience of disability that was not unequivocally positive, may have a sense of what needs to be and what can be managed. We have also seen how Mary found that high quality intervention at an early stage by good practitioners can enable a mother to have confidence both in herself and in her disabled child.

Many women, however, do not have those experiences to influence and sustain them when at birth or later, they find themselves the mother of a child that they were not expecting. Even those who do may find that it is not enough to offset entirely the impact of what they have to face. There are many reasons why a woman in such circumstances may feel desperate, including, for example, her fears and concerns about her child's health. Here, however, I wish to concentrate on the distressing and dislocating process of discovering what it means to become the mother of a child who is seen to belong to a socially excluded minority. For the women concerned, 'social exclusion' may not always be a familiar notion but nevertheless, there is no escaping the fact that they have become mothers of children who in the eyes of the majority, are firmly located on the other side of the track. There is no choice about crossing the divide and initially few signs to help them get their bearings in the unfamiliar place.

When negative perceptions about disability are so prevalent in the population as a whole, it is reasonable to assume that many women who find themselves mothers of disabled children initially approach the experience with at least some of the same attitudes that they later come to modify, reject and even despise. This was certainly the case for a number of the West Midlands mothers. As we have seen from the literature, however, through getting to know their children and finding themselves involved in the detail of a loving, caregiving relationship with them, women gradually change their minds not only about their particular child but about some aspects of disability generally. This is not of course to suggest that some mothers do not continue to wish that their children were without their impairments.

As she gets involved in a close relationship with her disabled child, it may become apparent to the woman that the two of them are not seen as having a rightful place in the world to which she had hitherto assumed that she belonged. The things that many others do and take for granted no longer seem to apply. Such things are suddenly beyond the reach of her and her child and they begin to find themselves in the category of the marginal and the exceptional in almost all respects.

Gregory (1991) describes for example how the content of popular baby and childcare manuals almost automatically excludes disabled children and their mothers right from the start. The reference to them is often limited to a list of useful addresses at the back of the book. Thus, a book that purports to be about children and child care per se, turns out actually to be about the upbringing of *some* children and not others. This is rarely spelled out however. It is simply taken as read that the category 'children' really means non-disabled children, while those who are disabled are assumed to be in a separate and exceptional grouping.

It is not only that the mother and her child are excluded ideologically and practically from such things as standard child care advice, information and provision, it is also that they and other members of the household may begin to experience a sense of social exclusion and ghettoization in both crude and subtle forms. The sense of now being in a different category seeps into their social relations at all levels and in most contexts. It happens in a way that goes beyond the making of arrangements which have to be in place to meet a child's particular needs.

More often than not, on the occasions when the mother and child are included in mainstream activities, they find that they do not quite fit. The circumstances and attitudes are not quite right and they may have the sense that they are guesting in a world or a part of it that is seen primarily to belong to others. Taking part in it may seem more like a concession than a right.

Through having a disabled child, the woman gradually discovers and experiences both directly and by proxy many of the oppressive aspects of society which disabled academics and activists have called to our attention during the past two decades. She may not always analyse or classify them in the same way as writers from the disabled people's movement but she experiences them nevertheless. Being the mother of a socially excluded child also inevitably brings with it at least some degree of secondary exclusion for her too.

As time progresses through the daily round with their children, the women continue to discover the unacceptable social consequences of being and of having a child living with impairment. In their own particular ways, in their own words and at their own pace, very many start to make a distinction between their child's impairment and the negative things that all too often go along with it in our contemporary society. Women who may never formally have heard of the 'social model of disability', become convinced through their own experience that many of the most restrictive features of their own and their children's lives are not an inevitable or necessary consequence of having impairments. They often believe that if only people were to regard it as important enough, many of those things could be changed and they and their children could have something different and better. As would be expected, there are a wide range of views on what would be desirable, how particular children's needs could be met and how their opportunities would be most effectively enhanced.

We have nevertheless seen from the body of empirical research, from books and articles written by mothers and from the accounts of the West Midlands women, the range of attitudes, material and environmental conditions, restricted opportunities and limitations in service provision that mothers believe work against their sons' and daughters' interests. Some come to believe that fundamentally their children are valued less than non-disabled children and that this explains the inequalities that they face. It can be argued that while there may be some differences of focus, expression and analysis, there is nevertheless considerable common ground between the mothers' accounts and those found in the broader literature on disability and oppression.

The mother accumulates, sifts and analyses raw and fragmented information about the unacceptable and distressing aspects of her own child's situation as she experiences it. She often comes to conclusions about it in relative isolation. As we have seen from earlier chapters, many do not have access to alternative information, support and advice. Essentially, therefore, the mother makes up her own mind, drawing on whatever information and opinion she can access. In some cases, this will include contributions from other members of her household.

Mothers also have to decide what to *do* about situations that need to be challenged or changed. Again, they may gain from the support and ideas of other family members but as we have already seen, their role as mothers is likely to mean that they are the people in their households who have probably accumulated most experience of sorting things out. They also have to make a lot of on the spot decisions as circumstances demand it. As was clear from the accounts of the West Midlands women, they sometimes felt unequal to the task and uncertain about the way forward. They were driven, however, by ideas or convictions about what was right and what was wrong. They spoke of things that in their view, *should* happen and things that could not be allowed to continue. They used the language of fairness and unfairness. They adopted a moral position and believed that no matter how inexperienced they felt, they had no alternative but to act for the sake of the child they loved.

The experience of mediation: hazards, dilemmas and positive achievements

Literature written by mothers of disabled children, accounts of the West Midlands mothers as well as other research give some indication of the wide range of mediation work that these women undertake. It takes place within their families, their neighbourhoods, in public places and in relation to essential services. In the face of widespread misunderstanding about disabled children, they may rarely feel off duty. As one of the West Midlands mothers explained, 'You are constantly presenting an alternative image of your child to the outside world . . . You are constantly changing their minds'. Alongside their attempts to change other people's hearts and minds, they also reinterpret events and ways of the world to their disabled sons and daughters and adopt proactive strategies to enhance their sense of well-being, self-worth and resiliance.

Doing all of this from a minority position, as well as from that of being a woman and a mother, is by no means easy. Resisting things that are usually taken as givens, from a position of relative social isolation and powerlessness, is always difficult. It carries with it a number of hazards of which the mothers concerned are only too aware. They quickly develop a working knowledge of what they are up against and whether they stand a chance of pulling off a result that is beneficial for the child.

While the past few years have undoubtedly witnessed improvements in the position and status of disabled people generally, there is, as we have seen, substantial evidence of the considerable barriers that are still ranged against them and the degree to which their civil rights are curtailed. Many of the things to which disabled children and adults and those close to them take exception, are very well established. They are embedded in the social fabric, they are built into the bricks and mortar of institutions and they are reinforced by dominant ideologies that are taken as natural and self-evident. Anyone resisting or challenging the everyday things, the allegedly self-evident things, may find themselves swimming against a very strong tide indeed.

Some of the examples that can be found in the literature and also in the accounts of the West Midlands women refer to mediation in relation to those matters related to health, social care and education, which were seen to have a major and lasting impact in their children's lives. In addition, attention has been drawn to demonstrate the imbalance of power that often exists between mothers and those whom they have to convince or challenge in the more formal service provision settings (e.g. Darling 1979; Strong 1979; Read 1985, 1991; Goodey 1991). It is not unlikely that Deborah's comment that she was 'only a mother', reflects quite widespread feelings that women have about their gender and status when they are in negotiation with professionals. The relative weakness of the women's position in a number of respects, and their awareness of it, influences their choice of strategy. They may sense that they need to be very diplomatic and not offend people whom they feel have the power to make crucial decisions in their child's life. It may also seem that in order to achieve something important, they sometimes have to emphasize certain characteristics of the child or the household. In doing so they may feel that they have to paint a particular picture of their child and their family that does not quite ring true. This can make them feel that they have misrepresented people who matter to them.

In doing all of this and more besides, they may sometimes have the uncomfortable feeling that they are paying more attention to the micropolitics of the situation, including the sensibilities of the more powerful professionals, than to what they regard as the real task in hand: the meeting of the child's needs. Many resent this process of keeping the balance right, the effort of keeping others sweet and the personal toll that it takes on them. One author and mother wrote of the sense of prostituting herself in order to achieve a goal (Lauruol 1998).

This work is enormously stressful and challenging for any mother and there is the ever-present worry about failure to achieve a particular aim on the child's behalf. As the research demonstrates, however, it is even harder for some than others. While all mothers may feel that they have to fight to make sure that the child's needs are fully represented and that they are not always in the strongest position to do it, some women and children who are from minority ethnic communities and on low incomes are in constant danger of being very marginalized (Sloper and Turner 1992; Baldwin and Carlisle 1994). The different facets of social exclusion, the extreme material restrictions and difficult life events with which many cope, mean that poor women and those from minority ethnic communities are often not in the position to mediate on their children's behalf in the way required to ensure success. Like Fazialt Jan, one of the West Midlands women, they may be well aware that something needs to be done and have to live with the knowledge that they could not make it happen no matter how hard they tried.

If mothers find that a balance has to be struck with service providers, the same is certainly true of those in the family, neighbourhood and among the general public who hold attitudes that the mothers see as damaging or insensitive to the child. A very great deal of the mediation they undertake is to do with the fine-grained stuff of the daily round within their families and neighbourhoods. While they may write off some people deemed to be particularly offensive or beyond redemption, much of the time they have to choose a different strategy. In the face of an attitude that they know is prevalent throughout society, particularly if it is held by someone whom they do not wish to offend, they have to make a diplomatic move that neither causes a rift nor sells the child short. Being a disabled child or their mother is isolated enough without being more cut off from family, neighbours and friends than is absolutely necessary.

In addition, there is the more sympathetic and personal stuff of mediation with the non-disabled sibling for whom the mother feels equal love and commitment. As we have seen, there is much explaining work as well as practical steps to be taken to ensure that fairness and justice are not only done but are seen to be done. An alternative explanation often has to be given in the face of the prejudiced views that the brother or sister encounters in the outside world and a practical strategy offered for dealing with them. In addition, there is also much listening to be done. Brothers and sisters may be sharp observers and good grass-roots theorists and strategists in their own right. It is not uncommon for mothers to comment upon the important insights about the disabled child that come out of the mouths of babes and siblings (e.g. Murray and Penman 1996).

A major part of mothers' mediating activities may consist of arguing their children in from the margins or putting them on the agenda in some way that is different from the existing place that they are seen to occupy. It is the changing of minds. Mothers often believe that they have knowledge, perspectives and insights of which others need to be convinced. That insight is gained through their close involvement with the child and through their knowledge of what life offers on the other side of the track. They often have a conviction that others who have not been there do not know what it is like and also that in many respects, it is not something of much significance to them.

Lauruol (1998) gave her account of a particular aspect of the isolating nature of discussions about your child with those who do not have a similar experience. In her view, having a disabled child has such a fundamental impact upon your life and your outlook that it changes you irrevocably. It also separates you from other people who do not have the experience and from the things that they take for granted. When others make reference to your experience, they frequently show that they misunderstand it quite fundamentally. The importance of your child, the things that you have learned and the impact of disability on your life, however, drive you to try to make them understand. Sadly, the very process of trying to explain and finding that people still cannot appreciate or accept the full meaning of what you are trying to say, can create an even greater barrier. It can also confirm your isolated and excluded position still further. Some mothers stop trying to explain everything and limit themselves to getting across the bare necessities that are needed to achieve a particular aim. Others, like Victoria from the West Midlands, refer wryly to the fact that they cannot help keep 'banging on'.

In a world which by and large does not operate in the interests of disabled children, we have seen that their mothers have to be extremely active negotiators if their needs are to be met. Becoming your child's active and successful negotiator, however, can lay the woman open to personal criticism. She may find herself caricatured as pushy and overbearing or stereotyped as the mother who has made an almost professional career out of being the parent of a disabled child. She may even be reproved, for example, for allegedly depriving other children of services by dint of her success at representing her own child's needs. It is not uncommon for disapproval and suspicion to be expressed about 'those who shout loudest'.

Such reactions may seem especially unfair to the mothers concerned. The women take on a very stressful and time-consuming activity because all the evidence that we and they have indicates that it needs to be done. If, in the face of Hobson's choice, they are successful at it and particularly if they acquire a taste for it, they may discover how quickly they can be pathologized. However much they dislike this, they may have to regard other people's opinions of them as being of lesser importance than achieving the desired outcome for the child.

Despite all the hazards and stresses that women detail, their accounts are also full of references to the fact that they have come a long way and made a great deal of progress. The process of change that they describe has enormously positive elements. Some of these are to do with the satisfaction and pleasure about things achieved with, for and by the child. They look at the progress that they supported their children to make and the negative influences that they managed to keep at bay. The West Midlands mothers' accounts of enabling children to develop resilience and a sense of ease with themselves in the face of difficult circumstances provide clear examples of achievements which they value. Mothers also relate the changes in their own attitudes which they see as positive. It is common for women to discuss how they came to have a different and more accepting view of disability through their loving and close relationship with the child. It is not unusual for them to feel that they have also absorbed knowledge and values that they think have a relevance beyond the immediate situation with their own son or daughter. Some take a delight in battles fought and won.

There is great diversity among women who have disabled children and it would be surprising were they all to come to identical conclusions about this particular experience of mothering and motherhood. Most, however, find unacceptable at least some aspects of what the status quo offers their sons and daughters and it is this that makes them so active in their role as mediators and allies on the ground.

Concluding comments

It seems fitting to give the last word to two women who have disabled children and who see themselves as their allies. Their experience of knowing their children led them to emphasize difference instead of deficit and social barriers in place of individual or medical restriction. While other mothers may have different perspectives, there can surely be few who would not recognize in elements of the two mothers' accounts a reflection of their own experience, intentions and motivation. Essentially the women concerned acknowledge how everything of importance that they have learned is grounded in their relationship with and knowledge of their children, built up over time. Their view of the world changes as a result of knowing the child. It is from that base that other crucial understandings develop, as does the imperative to challenge beliefs that are damaging to their sons' and daughters' well-being:

We are learning that the journey begins in our homes – in our own lives. We are learning to challenge the set of beliefs we grew up with. We are learning about being allies to our children. We write from a human rights perspective. We do not accept the medical or charitable models of disability which present our children as defective. They are models which we, as parents, are expected to accept and collude with against our children. To collude in this way would mean seeing our children in the negative way society at present sees them. This would fundamentally damage our relationships with our children. It would fundamentally damage our families . . . Our children are the ones who teach us about the issues. They give us the opportunities to learn and understand. They give us determination and confidence. They give us hope and courage. They show us how it can be done . . . Our children are teaching us how to be their allies.

(Murray and Penman 1996: ix)

References

Abberley, P. (1987) The concept of oppression and the development of a social theory of disability. *Disability, Handicap and Society*, 2(1): 5–19.

Abberley, P. (1992) Counting us out: a discussion of the OPCS disability surveys, *Disability, Handicap and Society*, 7(2): 139–55.

Abberley, P. (1996) Work, Utopia and impairment, in L. Barton (ed.) *Disability and Society: Emerging Issues and Insights*. London: Longman.

Abberley, P. (1997) The limits of classical social theory in the analysis and transformation of disablement – (Can this really be the end; to be stuck inside of Mobile with the Memphis blues again?), in L. Barton and M. Oliver (eds) *Disability Studies: Past, Present and Future*. Leeds: The Disability Press.

Abbott, P. and Sapsford, R. (1992) Leaving it to mum: 'community care' for mentally handicapped children, in P. Abbott and R. Sapsford (eds) *Research into Practice: A Reader for Nurses and the Caring Professions*. Buckingham: Open University Press.

Allen, J. (1981) Motherhood: the annihilation of women, in J. Treblicot (ed.) *Mothering: Essays in Feminist Theory*. Totowa, NJ: Rowman and Allenhead.

Anderson, H. (1995) *Disabled People and the Labour Market*. Birmingham: West Midlands Low Pay Unit.

Appleton, P., Boll, V., Everett, J., Kelly, A., Meredith, K. and Payne T. (1997) Beyond child development centres: care coordination for children with disabilities. *Child: Care, Health and Development*, 23(1): 29–40.

Appleton, P. and Minchom, P. (1991) Models of parent partnership and child development centres. *Child: Care, Health and Development*, 17: 27–38.

Atkin, K. (1992) Similarities and differences between informal carers, in J. Twigg (ed.) *Carers: Research and Practice*. London: HMSO.

Atkinson, N. and Crawforth, M. (1995) *All in the Family: Siblings and Disability*. London: NCH Action for Children.

Audit Commission (1992) *Getting in on the Act. Provision for Pupils with Special Educational Needs: The National Picture*. London: HMSO.

Audit Commission (1994) *Seen But Not Heard: Coordinating Community Child Health and Social Services for Children in Need*. London: HMSO.

Badinter, E. (1981) *The Myth of Motherhood: An Historical View of the Maternal Instinct*. London: Souvenir Press.

Baldwin, S. (1985) *The Costs of Caring: Families with Disabled Children*. London: Routledge and Kegan Paul.

Baldwin, S. and Carlisle, J. (1994) *Social Support for Disabled Children and Their Families: A Review of the Literature*. Edinburgh: HMSO.

Baldwin, S. and Glendinning, C. (1981) Children with disabilities and their families, in A. Walker and P. Townsend (eds) *Disability in Britain: A Manifesto of Rights*. Oxford: Martin Robertson.

Baldwin, S. and Glendinning, C. (1983) Employment, women and their disabled children, in A. Walker and P. Townsend (eds) *Disability in Britain: A Manifesto of Rights*. Oxford: Martin Robertson.

Ballard, K., Bray, A., Sheton, E. and Clarkson, J. (1997) Children with disabilities and the education system: the experiences of fifteen fathers. *International Journal of Disability, Development and Education*, 44(3): 229–41.

Barnes, C. (1991) *Disabled People in Britain and Discrimination*. London: Hurst & Co, in association with the British Council of Organisations of Disabled People.

Barnes, C. (1997) A legacy of oppression: a history of disability in western culture, in L. Barton and M. Oliver (eds) *Disability Studies: Past, Present and Future*. Leeds: The Disability Press.

Barnes, C. and Mercer, G. (eds) (1996) *Exploring the Divide: Illness and Disability*. Leeds: The Disability Press.

Barnes, C. and Mercer, G. (1997) Breaking the mould? an introduction to doing disability research, in C. Barnes and G. Mercer (eds) *Doing Disability Research*. Leeds: The Disability Press.

Bart, P. (1983) Review of Chodorow's *The Reproduction of Mothering*, in J. Treblicot (ed.) *Mothering: Essays in Feminist Theory*. Totowa, NJ: Rowman and Allenhead.

Barton, L. (1986) The politics of special educational needs, *Disability, Handicap and Society*, 1(3): 273–90.

Barton, L. (1987) *The Politics of Special Educational Needs*. London: Falmer Press.

Barton, L. (1996) Sociology and disability: some emerging issues, in L. Barton (ed.) *Disability and Society: Emerging Issues and Insights*. London: Longman.

Baxter, C., Kamarjit, P., Ward, L. and Nadirshaw, Z. (1990) *Double Discrimination: Issues and Services for People with Learning Difficulties from Black and Ethnic Minority Communities*. London: Kings Fund Centre.

BBC (1998) Here and Now. Manchester, 1 June.

Beardshaw, V. (1989) Conductive education: a rejoinder. *Disability, Handicap and Society*, 4(3): 297–9.

Begum, N. (1990) *The Burden of Gratitude: Women with Disabilities Receiving Personal Care*. University of Warwick: Social Care Practice Centre/Department of Applied Social Studies.

Begum, N. (1992) *Something to Be Proud of: The Lives of Asian Disabled People and Carers in Waltham Forest*. London: Waltham Forest Race Relations Unit and Disability Unit.

Begum, N., Hill, M. and Stevens, A. (1994) *Reflections: The Views of Black Disabled People on their Lives and Community Care*. London: CCETSW.

Belenky, M., Blythe, C., Goldberger, N. and Tarule, J. (1986) *Women's Ways of Knowing*. New York: Basic Books.

Benn, C. (1998) *Madonna and Child: Towards a New Politics of Motherhood*. London: Jonathan Cape.

Beresford, B. (1994) *Positively Parents: Caring for a Severely Disabled Child*. London: HMSO.

Beresford, B. (1995) *Expert Opinions: A National Survey of Parents Caring for a Severely*

Disabled Child. Bristol: The Policy Press, in association with the Joseph Rowntree Foundation and Community Care.

Beresford, B. (1997) *Personal Accounts: Involving Disabled Children in Research*. London: HMSO.

Beresford, B., Sloper, P., Baldwin, S. and Newman, T. (1996) *What Works in Services for Families with a Disabled Child*. Barkingside: Barnardos.

Bertoud, R., Lakey, J. and McKay, S. (1993) *The Economic Problems of Disabled People*. London: Policy Studies Institute.

Billis, D. and Harris, M. (eds) (1996) *Voluntary Agencies: Challenges of Organisation and Management*. Basingstoke: Macmillan.

Blackburn, C. (1991) *Poverty and Health: Working with Families*. Buckingham: Open University Press.

Blaxter, M. (1976) *The Meaning of Disability*. London: Heinemann.

Booth, T. (1992) *Reading Critically, Unit 10, E241*. Milton Keynes: The Open University.

Booth, T., Swann, W., Masterson, M. and Potts, P. (1992) (eds) *Curricula for Diversity in Education*. London: Routledge in association with The Open University.

Bortolaia Silva, E. (1996) The transformation of mothering, in E. Bortolaia Silva (ed.) *Good Enough Mothering?: Feminist Perspectives on Lone Motherhood*. London: Routledge.

Boston, S. (1981) *Will, My Son*. London: Pluto Press.

Bowlby, J. (1951) *Maternal Care and Mental Health*. Geneva: World Health Organization.

Bradshaw, J. (1980) *The Family Fund: An Initiative in Social Policy*. London: Routledge and Kegan Paul.

Bradshaw, J., Baldwin, S. and Glendinning, C. (1977) Services that miss their mark and leave families in need, *Health and Social Services Journal*, April: 664–5.

Bury, M. (1996) Defining and researching disability: challenges and responses, in C. Barnes and G. Mercer (eds) *Exploring the Divide: Illness and Disability*. Leeds: The Disability Press.

Butler, N., Gill, R., Pomeroy, D. and Fewtrell, J. (1977) How do they manage? *Housing Review*, November: 143–6.

Butt, J. and Mirza, K. (1996) *Social Care and Black Communities*. London: HMSO.

Bynoe, I., Oliver, M. and Barnes, C. (1991) *Equal Rights for Disabled People*. London: Institute for Public Policy Research.

Campling, J. (ed.) (1981) *Images of Ourselves: Women with Disabilities Talking*. London: Routledge & Kegan Paul.

Cantwell, P., Baker, L. and Rutter, M. (1978) Family factors, in M. Rutter and E. Scheppler (eds) *Autism, a Reappraisal of Concepts and Treatment*. New York: Plenum Press.

Chodorow, N. (1978) *The Reproduction of Mothering: Psychoanalysis and the Sociology of Gender*. Berkeley, CA: University of California Press.

Clarke, P., Kofsky, H. and Lauruol, J. (1989) *To a Different Drumbeat*. Stroud: Hawthorn Press.

Clements, L. (1996) *Community Care and the Law*. London: Legal Action Group.

Cochrane, A. (1993) *Whatever Happened to Local Government?* Buckingham: Open University Press.

Corbett, J. (1994) A proud label: exploring the relationship between disability politics and gay pride, *Disability Society*, 9(3): 343–57.

Corrigan, P. (1979) *Schooling the Smash Street Kids*. London: Macmillan.

Cronin, P. and Fullwood, D. (1986) *Facing the Crowd*. Melbourne: Royal Victorian Institute for the Blind.

Crow, L. (1996) Including all of our lives, in J. Morris (ed.) *Encounters with Strangers: Feminism and Disability*. London: The Women's Press.

Cunningham, C. (1983) Early support and intervention: the HARC infant project, in P. Mittler and H. McConnachie (eds) *Parents, Professionals and Mentally Handicapped People: Approaches to Partnership*. London: Croom Helm.

Dalrymple, J. and Burke, B. (1995) *Anti-oppressive Practice: Social Care and the Law*. Buckingham: Open University Press.

Darling, R.B. (1979) *Families Against Society*. Beverly Hills, CA: Sage Publications Inc.

DHSS (Department of Health and Social Security) (1969) *Report of the Committee of Enquiry into Allegations of Ill-treatment and Other Irregularities at Ely Hospital, Cardiff* (Howe Report) Cmnd 3785. London: HMSO.

DES (1978) *The Report of the Committee of Enquiry into the Education of Handicapped Children and Young People* (Warnock Report), Cmnd 7212. London: HMSO.

DHSS (Department of Health and Social Security) (1971) *Better Services for the Mentally Handicapped*, Cmnd 4683. London: HMSO.

DHSS (Department of Health and Social Security) (1976) *Fit for the Future: The Report of the Committee on Child Health Services* (Court Report), Cmnd 6684. London: HMSO.

DoH (Department of Health) (1995) *Child Protection: Messages From Research*. London: HMSO.

Dyson, S. (1992) Blood relations: educational implications of sickle-cell anaemia and thalassaemia, in T. Booth, W. Swann, M. Masterso and P. Potts (eds) *Curricula for Diversity in Education*. London: Routledge in association with The Open University.

Dyson, S. (1998) 'Race', ethnicity and haemoglobin disorders. *Social Science and Medicine*. 47(1): 121–31.

Everingham, C. (1994) *Motherhood and Modernity: An Investigation into the Rational Dimensions of Mothering*. Buckingham: Open University Press.

Family Focus (1983) Parents underrated but undeterred. *Special Education: Forward Trends*. 10(4): 27–8.

Family Focus (1984) *Swimming Against the Tide: Working for Integration in Education*. Coventry: Coventry Resource and Information Service.

Finch, J. (1989) *Family Obligations and Social Change*. Cambridge: Polity Press.

Finch, J. and Groves, D. (eds) (1980) *A Labour of Love: Women, Work and Caring*. London: Routledge and Kegan Paul.

Finger, A. (1991) *Past Due: A Story of Disability, Pregnancy and Birth*. London: The Women's Press.

Finkelstein, V. (1980) *Attitudes and Disabled People: Issues for Discussion*. New York: World Rehabilitation Fund.

Firestone, S. (1972) *The Dialectic of Sex*. London: Paladin.

Flynn, M. and Hurst, M. (1992) *This Year, Next Year, Sometime . . . ? Learning Disability and Adulthood*. London: National Development Team.

French, S. (1993) Disability, impairment or something in between? in J. Swain, V. Finkelstein, S. French and M. Oliver (eds) *Disabling Barriers – Enabling Environments*. London: Sage Publications, in association with The Open University.

French, S. (1994a) What is disability? in S. French (ed.) *On Equal Terms*. London: Butterworth and Heinemann.

French, S. (1994b) Disabled people and professional practice, in S. French (ed.) *On Equal Terms*. London: Butterworth and Heinemann.

French, S. (1996) Out of sight, out of mind: the experience and effects of a 'special' residential school, in J. Morris (ed.) *Encounters with Strangers: Feminism and Disability*. London: The Women's Press.

Friedan, B. (1963) *The Feminine Mystique*. London: Victor Gollancz.

Friedan, B. (1981) *The Second Stage*. New York: Summit Books.

Gieve, K. (ed.) (1989) *Balancing Acts: On Being a Mother*. London: Virago.

Gilligan, C. (1982) *In a Different Voice: Psychological Theory and Women's Development*. Cambridge, MA: Harvard University Press.

Glendinning, C. (1983) *Unshared Care: Parents and Their Disabled Children*. London: Routledge and Kegan Paul.

Glendinning, C. (1986) *A Single Door: Social Work with Families of Disabled Children*. London: Allen & Unwin.

Glenn, E. (1994) Social constructions of mothering, in E. Glenn, G. Chang and L. Forcey (eds) *Mothering: Ideology, Experience and Agency*. New York: Routledge.

Gliedman, J. and Roth, W. (1980) *The Unexpected Minority: Handicapped Children in America*. New York: Harcourt Brace Jovanovich.

Goodey, C. (1991) *Living in the Real World: Families Speak about Down's Syndrome*. London: The Twenty–One Press.

Goodey, C. (1992) Fools and heretics: parents' views of professionals, in T. Booth, M. Masterson, P. Potts and W. Swann (eds) *Policies for Diversity in Education*. London: Routledge in association with The Open University.

Gooding, C. (1994) *Disabling Laws, Enabling Acts: Disability Rights in Britain and America*. London: Pluto Press.

Goodison, L. (1981) Only they know how it feels, *Mind Out*, September: 13–15.

Gough, D., Li, L. and Wroblewska, A. (1993) *Services for Children with a Motor Impairment and Their Families in Scotland*, Glasgow: Public Health Research Unit, University of Glasgow.

Graham, H. (1977) Women's attitudes to conception and pregnancy, in R. Chester and J. Peel (eds) *Equalities and Inequalities in Family Life*. London: Academic Press.

Graham, H. (1980) Mothers' accounts of anger and aggression towards their babies, in N. Frude (ed.) *Psychological Approaches to Child Abuse*. London: Batsford.

Graham, H. (1982) Coping: or how mothers are seen and not heard, in S. Friedman and E. Sarah (eds) *On the Problem of Men: Two Feminist Conferences*. London: The Women's Press.

Graham, H. (1984) *Women, Health and the Family*. Brighton: Wheatsheaf Books.

Graham, H. (1985) Providers, negotiators and mediators: women as the hidden carers, in E. Lewin (ed.) *Women, Health and Healing: Towards a New Perspective*. New York: Tavistock.

Graham, H. (1993a) Social divisions in caring. *Women's Studies International Forum*, 16(5): 461–70.

Graham, H. (1993b) *Hardship and Health in Women's Lives*. Brighton: Harvester Wheatsheaf.

Graham, H. and Oakley, A. (1981) Competing ideologies of reproduction: medical and maternal perspectives on pregnancy, in H. Roberts (ed.) *Women, Health and Reproduction*. London: Routledge and Kegan Paul.

Greer, G. (1971) *The Female Eunuch*. London: Paladin.

Gregory, S (1991) Challenging motherhood: mothers and their deaf children, in A. Phoenix, A. Woollett and E. Lloyd (eds) *Motherhood, Meanings and Practices*. London: Sage Publications.

Griffiths, Sir R. (1988) *Community Care: Agenda for Action*. London: HMSO.

Gunarantam, Y. (1993) Breaking the silence: Asian carers in Britain, in J. Bornat, C. Pereira, D. Pilgrim and F. Williams (eds) *Community Care: A Reader*. Basingstoke: Macmillan.

Gupta, R (1989) Giving birth again, in K. Gieve (ed.) *Balancing Acts: On Being a Mother*. London: Virago.

Hall, D. (1997) Child development teams: are they fulfilling their purpose? *Child Care, Health and Development*, 23(1): 87–99.

Hannaford, S. (1985) *Living on the Outside Inside*. Berkeley, CA: Canterbury Press.

Hannam, C. (1975) *Parents and Mentally Handicapped Children*. London: Penguin Books, in association with Mind.

Haylock, C., Johnson, A. and Harpin, V. (1993) Parents' views of community care for children with motor disabilities, *Child: Care, Health and Development*, 19: 209–20.

Hevey, D. (1992) *The Creatures Time Forgot*. London: Routledge.

Hewett, S. (1970) *The Family and the Handicapped Child*. London: Allen & Unwin.

Hewett, S. (1976) Research on families with handicapped children – an aid or an impediment to understanding, *Birth Defects*, XII, 34–5.

Hirsh, M. and Fox Keller, E. (1990) *Conflicts in Feminism*. New York: Routledge.

Hirst, M. (1991) Dissolution and reconstitution of families with a disabled young person, *Developmental Medicine and Child Neurology*, 33: 1073–9.

Hirst, M. and Baldwin, S. (1994) *Unequal Opportunities*. London: HMSO.

Holliday, I. (1992) *The NHS Transformed*. Manchester: Baseline Books.

Hubert, J. (1993) At home and alone: families and young adults with challenging behaviour, in J. Bornat, C. Pereira, D. Pilgrim and F. Williams (eds) *Community Care: A Reader*. Basingstoke: Macmillan, in association with The Open University.

Humphries, S. and Gordon, P. (1992) *Out of Sight: the Experience of Disability 1900–1950*. Plymouth: Northcote House Publishers.

Kaplan, E.A. (1992) *Motherhood and Representation*. London: Routledge.

Keith, L. (1994) (ed.) *Mustn't Grumble: Writing by Disabled Women*. London: The Women's Press.

Keith, L. (1996) Encounters with strangers: the public's response to disabled women and how this affects our sense of self, in J. Morris (ed.) *Encounters with Strangers: Feminism and Disability*. London: The Women's Press.

Kennedy, M. (1992) Not the only way to communicate: a challenge to the voice in child protection work, *Child Abuse Review*, 1: 169–77.

Kennedy, M. (1996) The sexual abuse of disabled children, in J. Morris (ed.) *Encounters with Strangers: Feminism and Disability*. London: The Women's Press.

Langan, M. and Day, L. (eds) (1992) *Women, Oppression and Social Work Issues in Anti-discriminatory Practice*. London: Routledge.

Lauruol, J. (1998) Personal correspondence.

Lawton, D. (1989) Very young children and the Family Fund, *Children and Society*, 3(3): 212–25.

Leonard, P. (1984) *Personality and Ideology*. Basingstoke: Macmillan.

Lewis, A. (1995) *Children's Understanding of Disability*. London: Routledge.

Lonsdale, S. (1990) *Women and Disability*. Basingstoke: Macmillan.

Low, C. (1996) Disability models or muddles? *Therapy Weekly*, 22(30): 7.

McCarthy, M. (ed.) (1989) *The New Politics of Welfare: An Agenda for the 1990s?* Basingstoke: Macmillan.

McConachie, H. (1997) The organisation of child disability services, *Child Care, Health and Development*, 23(1): 3–9.

MacHeath, C. (1992) Maresa, in J. Morris (ed.) *Alone Together: Voices of Single Mothers*. London: The Women's Press.

McNay, L. (1992) *Foucault and Feminism*. Cambridge: Polity Press.

Marchant, R. and Page, M. (1992) Bridging the gap: investigating the abuse of children with multiple disabilities, *Child Abuse Review*, 1: 179–83.

Mason, M. (1992) A nineteen parent family, in Morris, J. (ed.) *Alone Together: Voices of Single Mothers*. London: The Women's Press.

Mayall, B. (1996) *Children, Health and the Social Order*. Buckingham: Open University Press.

Meltzer, H., Smyth, M. and Robus, N. (1989) *Disabled Children: Services, Transport and Education, Report 6*. London: HMSO.

Millett, K. (1970) *Sexual Politics*. New York: Doubleday.

Minkes, J., Robinson, C. and Weston, C. (1994) Consulting the child: interviews with children using residential respite services, *Disability and Society*, 9(1): 561–71.

Mitchell, J. (1974) *Psychoanalysis and Feminism*. London: Allen Lane.

Mittler, P. and McConachie, H. (1983) *Parents, Professionals and Mentally Handicapped People: Approaches to Partnership*. London: Croom Helm.

Morgan, D. (1996) *Family Connections*. Cambridge: Polity Press.

Morris, J. (1989) *Able Lives: Women's Experience of Paralysis*. London: The Women's Press.

Morris, J. (ed.) (1991) *Pride Against Prejudice*. London: The Women's Press.

Morris J. (ed.) (1992) *Alone Together: Voices of Single Mothers*. London: The Women's Press.

Morris, J. (1993a) *Independent Lives: Community Care and Disabled People*. Basingstoke: Macmillan.

Morris, J. (1993b) 'Us' and 'them'? feminist research and community care, in J. Bornat, C. Pereira, D. Pilgrim and F. Williams (eds) *Community Care: A Reader*. Basingstoke: Macmillan, in association with The Open University.

Morris, J. (1994) Gender and disability, in S. French (ed.) *On Equal Terms*. London: Butterworth and Heinemann.

Morris, J. (1995) *Gone Missing? A Research and Policy Review of Disabled Children Living Away from their Families*. London: The Who Cares Trust.

Morris, J. (ed.) (1996) *Encounters with Strangers: Feminism and Disability*. London: The Women's Press.

Morris, J. (1998) *Accessing Human Rights: Disabled Children and the Children Act*. Barkingside: Barnardos.

Murray, P. (1992) Jessie and Kim, in J. Morris (ed.) *Alone Together: Voices of Single Mothers*. London: The Women's Press.

Murray, P. and Penman, J. (1996) *Let Our Children Be*. Sheffield: Parents with Attitude.

NACAB (1994) *Unequal Opportunities: CAB Evidence on Discrimination in Employment*. London: National Association of Citizens Advice Bureaux.

Newson, E. (1981) Parents as a resource in diagnosis and assessment, in A. Brechin, P. Liddiard and J. Swain (eds) *Handicap in a Social World*. London: Hodder and Stoughton, in association with The Open University.

O'Connor, N. and Ryan, J. (1993) *Wild Desires and Mistaken Identities: Lesbianism and Psychoanalysis*. London: Virago.

Oliver, M. (1983) *Social Work with Disabled People*. London: Macmillan.

Oliver, M. (1985) Discrimination, disability and social policy, in M. Brenton and C. Jones (eds) *The Yearbook of Social Policy 1984–5*. London: Routledge and Kegan Paul.

Oliver, M. (1990) *The Politics of Disablement*. London: Macmillan.

Oliver, M. (1992) Changing the social relations of research production, *Disability, Handicap and Society*, 7(2): 101–14.

Oliver, M. (1996) *Understanding Disability*. London: Macmillan.

OPCS (Office of Population, Censuses and Surveys) (1989) *Surveys of Disability in Britain*. London: HMSO.

Oswin, M. (1971) *The Empty Hours*. London: Allen Lane The Penguin Press.

Oswin, M. (1978) *Children Living in Long-Stay Hospitals*. London: Spastics International/Heinemann.

Oswin, M. (1984) *They Keep Going Away*. London: King Edward Hospital Fund for London.

Oswin, M (1998) A historical perspective, in C. Robinson and K. Stalker (eds) *Growing Up with Disability*. London: Jessica Kingsley Publishers.

Pahl, J. (1988) Earning, sharing, spending: married couples and their money, in R. Walker and G. Parker (eds) *Money Matters: Income, Wealth and Financial Welfare*. London: Sage Publications.

Pahl, J. and Quine, E. (1986) First diagnosis of severe mental handicap: characteristics of unsatisfactory encounters between doctors and parents, *Social Science and Medicine*, 22: 53–62.

Parker, G. and Lawton, D. (1994) *Different Types of Care, Different Types of Carer: Evidence from the General Household Survey*. London: HMSO.

Philp, M. and Duckworth, D. (1982) *Children with Disabilities and their Families: a Review of Research*. Windsor: NFER/Nelson.

Phoenix, A. and Woollett, A. (1991a) Introduction, in A. Phoenix, A. Woollett and E. Lloyd (eds) *Motherhood, Meanings, Practices and Ideologies*. London: Sage Publications.

Phoenix, A. and Woollett, A. (1991b) Motherhood: social construction, politics and psychology, in A. Phoenix, A.Woollett and E. Lloyd (eds) *Motherhood, Meanings, Practices and Ideologies*. London: Sage Publications.

Pinder, R. (1996) Sick-but-fit or fit-but-sick? ambiguity and identity at the workplace, in C. Barnes and G. Mercer (eds) *Exploring the Divide: Illness and Disability*. Leeds: The Disability Press.

Pitkeathly, J. (1989) *It's My Duty, Isn't It? The Plight of Carers in Our Society*. London: Souvenir Press.

Pollert, A. (1981) *Girls, Wives, Factory Lives*. London: Macmillan.

Potts, P. (1983) What difference would integration make to professionals? in T. Booth and P. Potts (eds) *Integrating Special Education*. Basil Blackwell: Oxford.

Priestley, M. (1998) Childhood disability and disabled childhoods: agendas for research, *Childhood* 5(2): 207–23.

Read, J. (1985) A critical appraisal of the concept of partnership: reflections on the working relationship between professionals and parents who have children with disabilities. Unpublished MA thesis, University of Warwick.

Read, J. (1987) The structural position of mentally handicapped adults, children and their carers: some implications for practice, in CCETSW, *Policy, Politics and Practice: Training for Work with Mentally Handicapped People*. Rugby: Central Council for Education and Training in Social Work.

Read, J. (1991) There was never really any choice: the experience of mothers of disabled children in the United Kingdom, *Women's Studies International Forum*, 14(6): 561–71.

Read, J. (1998) Conductive education and the politics of disablement, *Disability and Society*, 13(2): 279–93.

Read, J. and Statham, J. (1998) The preschool years, in C. Robinson and K. Stalker (eds) *Growing up with Disability*. London: Jessica Kingsley Publishers.

Reisser, R. (1992) Internalised oppression, how it seems to me, in T. Booth, W. Swann, M. Masterson and P. Potts (eds) *Policies for Diversity in Education*. London: Routledge, in association with The Open University.

Reisser, R. and Mason, M. (1992) *Disability Equality in the Classroom*. London: Disability Equality in Education.

Riley, D. (1983) *The War in the Nursery*. London: Virago.

Robinson, C. (1998) Breaks for disabled children, in K. Stalker (ed.) *Developments in Short-term Care: Breaks and Opportunities*. London: Jessica Kingsley Publishers.

Rogers, R. (1986a) *Caught in the Act*. London: CSIE, The Spastics Society.

Rogers, R. (1986b) *Guiding the Professionals*. London: CSIE, The Spastics Society.

Roith, A. (1974) The myth of parental attitudes, in D. Boswell and J. Wingrove (eds) *The Handicapped Person in the Community*. London: Tavistock Publications for The Open University.

Ruddick, S. (1989) *Maternal Thinking*. New York: Ballantine.

Russell, P. (1991) Working with children with physical disabilities and their families: the social work role, in M. Oliver (ed.) *Social Work, Disabled People and Disabling Environments*. London: Jessica Kingsley Publishers.

Rutter, M. (1972) *Maternal Deprivation Reassessed*. Harmondsworth: Penguin Books.

Ryan, J. and Thomas, F. (1980) *The Politics of Mental Handicap*. London: Penguin Books.

Saxton, M. and Howe, F. (eds) (1988) *With Wings: An Anthology of Literature by Women with Disabilities*. London: Virago.

Shah, R. (1992) *The Silent Minority: Children with Disabilities in Asian Families*. London: National Children's Bureau.

Shah, R. (1997) Services for Asian families and children with disabilities, *Child: Care, Health and Development*, 23(1): 41–6.

Shakespeare, T. (1994) Cultural representations of disabled people: dustbins for disavowal, *Disability and Society*, 9(3): 283–301.

Shakespeare, T. (1996) Disability, identity and difference, in C. Barnes and D. Mercer (eds) *Exploring the Divide*. Leeds: The Disability Press.

Shakespeare, T., Gillespie-Sells, K. and Davies, D. (1996) *The Sexual Politics of Disability*. London: Cassell.

Shearer, A. (1980) *Disability: Whose Handicap?* Oxford: Blackwell.

Shearer, A. (1984) *Everybody's Ethics: What Future for Handicapped Babies?* London: The Campaign for Mentally Handicapped People.

Sheik, S. (1986) An Asian mothers' self-help group, in S. Ahmed, J. Cheetham and J. Small (eds) *Social Work with Black Children and their Families*. London: Batsford.

Sheldon, B. (1994) The social and biological components of mental disorder: implications for services, *International Journal of Social Psychiatry*, 40(2): 87–105.

Sloper, P. and Turner, S. (1982) Service needs of families of children with severe physical disability, *Child Care, Health and Development*, 18: 259–82.

Sloper, P. and Turner, S. (1992) Service needs of families of children with severe physical disability, *Child: Care, Health and Development*, 18: 259–82.

Smart, C. (1996) Deconstructing motherhood, in E. Bortolaia Silva (ed.) *Good Enough Mothering?: Feminist Perspectives on Lone Motherhood*. London: Routledge.

Smith, A. (1994) Damaging experience: black disabled children and educational and social services provision, in N. Begum, M. Hill and A. Stevens (eds) *Reflections: the Views of Black Disabled People on their Lives and Community Care*. London: CCETSW.

Smith, A. (1998) *I'm Used to It Now: Disabled Women in Residential Care*. London: Greater London Association of Disabled People.

Smith, M. (1989) The best of all worlds? in K. Gieve (ed.) *Balancing Acts: On Being a Mother*. London: Virago.

Smith, M. and Robus, N. (1989) *The Financial Circumstances of Families with Disabled Children Living in Private Households*, Report 5. London: HMSO.

Social Services Inspectorate (1994) *Services to Disabled Children and their Families: Report of the National Inspection of Services to Disabled Children and their Families*. London: HMSO.

Stacey, M. (1980) Charisma, power and altruism: a discussion of research in a child development centre, *Sociology of Health and Illness*, 2(1): 64–90.

Stallard, P. and Lenton, S. (1992) How satisfied are parents of pre-school children who have special needs with services they have received? A consumer survey, *Child: Care, Health and Development*, 18: 197–205.

Stevens, A. (1991) *Disability Issues: Developing Anti-discriminatory Practice*. London: Central Council for Education and Training in Social Work.

Strong, P. (1979) *The Ceremonial Order of the Clinic, Doctors and Medical Bureaucracies*. London: Routledge and Kegan Paul.

Stuart, O. (1993) Double oppression: an appropriate starting point, in J. Swain, V. Finkelstein, S. French and M. Oliver (eds) *Disabling Barriers – Enabling Environments*. London: Sage Publications, in association with The Open University.

Sutherland, A. (1981) *Disabled We Stand*. London: Souvenir Press.

Thomas, C. (1997) The baby and the bath water: disabled women and motherhood in social context, *Sociology of Health and Illness*, 19(5): 622–43.

Thomas, D. (1982) *The Experience of Handicap*. London: Methuen.

Thompson, N. (1993) *Anti-discriminatory Practice*. London: Macmillan.

Thornton, P., Sainsbury, R. and Barnes H. (1997) *Helping Disabled People to Work: A Cross-National Study of Social Security and Employment Provisions. A Report for the Social Security Advisory Committee*. London: The Stationery Office.

Tippett, J. (1990) Sophie Tippett, in J. Read (ed.) *Conductive Education?* Birmingham: Foundation for Conductive Education.

Tomlinson, S. (1982) *A Sociology of Special Education*. London: Routledge & Kegan Paul.

Traustadottir, R. (1991) Mothers who care: gender, disability and family life, *Journal of Family Issues*, 12(2): 211–28.

Treblicot, J. (1983) *Mothering: Essays in Feminist Theory*. Totowa, NJ: Rowman and Allenhead.

Twigg, J. and Atkin, K. (1993) *Policy and Practice in Informal Care*. Buckingham: Open University Press.

Twigg, J. and Atkin, K. (1994) *Carers Perceived: Policy and Practice in Informal Care*. Buckingham: Open University Press.

Tyne, A. (1982) Community care and mentally handicapped people, in A.Walker (ed.) *Community Care: the Family, the State and Social Policy*. Oxford: Basil Blackwell and Martin Robertson.

UPIAS (1976) *Fundamental Principles of Disability*. London: Union of the Physically Impaired Against Segregation.

Walker, A. (1980) The social origins of impairment, disability and handicap, *Medicine and Society*, 6(2): 18–26.

Walker, A. (1982) *Unqualified and Underemployed. Handicapped Young People in the Labour Market*. London: Macmillan.

Ward, L. (1997a) Funding for change: translating emancipatory disability research from theory to practice, in C. Barnes and G. Mercer (eds) *Doing Disability Research*. Leeds: The Disability Press.

Ward, L. (1997b) *Seen and Heard: Involving Disabled Children and Young People in Research and Development Projects*. York: Joseph Rowntree Foundation.

WHO (World Health Organization) (1980) *The International Classification of Impairments, Disabilities and Handicaps*. Geneva: WHO.

Wilkin, D. (1979) *Caring for the Mentally Handicapped Child*. London: Croom Helm.

Williams, E. (1992) One hundred thousand families to support, *Search*, 13, September: 17–19.

Williams, F. (1993) Women and community, in J. Bornat, C. Pereira, D. Pilgrim and F. Williams (eds) *Community Care: A Reader*. Basingstoke: Macmillan.

Williams, G. (1996) Representing disabilities: some questions of phenomenology and politics, in C. Barnes and G. Mercer (eds) *Exploring the Divide: Illness and Disability.* Leeds: The Disability Press.

Willis, P. (1978) *Learning to Labour: How Working Class Kids Get Working Class Jobs.* London: Saxon House.

Winnicott, D. (1964) *The Child, the Family, and the Outside World.* Harmondsworth: Penguin Books.

Wishart, J., MacLeod, H. and Rowan, C. (1993) Parents' evaluations of pre-school services for children with Down's syndrome in two Scottish regions, *Child: Care, Health and Development*, 19: 1–23.

Woollett, A. and Phoenix, A. (1991) Afterword: issues related to motherhood, in A. Phoenix and A. Woollett (eds) *Motherhood, Meanings and Practices.* London: Sage Publications.

Yerbury, M. (1997) Issues in multidisciplinary teamwork for children with disabilities. *Child: Care, Health and Development*, 23(1): 77–86.

Younghusband, E., Birchall, D., Davie, R. and Kellmer Pringle, M.L. (1970) *Living with Handicap.* London: National Children's Bureau.

Index

ENABLING TECHNOLOGY
DISABLED PEOPLE, WORK AND NEW TECHNOLOGY

Alan Roulstone

- What is the significance of new microchip technologies for disabled workers/ job seekers?
- How is new technology enabling some disabled workers to gain enhanced access to employment and a more enabling employment?
- What are the policy implications of the research findings and the re-evaluation of the role of new technology?

There is much evidence to suggest that disabled people are less likely to be afforded the same rights as able-bodied workers in accessing jobs, equal employment rights and equal access to the workplace. Using a social barriers model of disability, *Enabling Technology* addresses the role of new technology in reducing the environmental and attitude barriers disabled people have commonly faced in the field of employment. This work is critical of established writings on disability and new technology and suggests that by adopting a medical model of disability such analyses have misrepresented the benefits of new technology for disabled people. A social barriers model views the benefits of new technology as inhering in its potential to rehabilitate disabling environments. The book addresses the urgent need to reframe policies on technology access away from a welfarist 'eligibility' model to a 'social rights' approach, one where disabled people are centrally involved in the framing, operation and review of technology access policy.

Enabling Technology is recommended reading for students and researchers in disability studies, applied social sciences and the sociology of work. It is also of relevance to those working in rehabilitation medicine and occupational therapy.

Contents

176pp   0 335 19801 5 (Paperback)   0 335 19802 3 (Hardback)

TALKING ABOUT APHASIA

Susie Parr, Sally Byng and Sue Gilpin with Chris Ireland

What is aphasia actually like – for those who have lost language, and those around them? What impact does it have on people's lives? Can the fearful communication gap somehow be bridged? Here is a book which addresses these questions and innumerable other related issues, with the most meticulous research and the most accessible descriptions. *Talking About Aphasia* will be equally valuable for professionals and patients alike, as well as the families, friends and therapists of those with aphasia.

Oliver Sacks

This book is a wonderful idea and it meets a heretofore unmet need. It derives from a particularly interesting database, since it deals with aphasia in aphasic people's own language . . . It is strongly recommended.

Professor Audrey Holland, Department of
Speech Pathology, University of Arizona, USA

This book is about living with aphasia – a language impairment which can result from stroke. Drawing on in-depth interviews with fifty aphasic people, it explores the experience of aphasia from the dramatic onset of stroke and loss of language to the gradual revelation of its long-term consequences. The story is told from the perspective of aphasic people themselves. They describe the impact of aphasia upon their employment, education, leisure activities, finances, personal relationships and identity. They describe their changing needs and how well these have been met by health, social care and other services. They talk about what aphasia means to them, the barriers encountered in everyday life and how they cope. The book offers a unique insight into the struggle of living with aphasia, combining startlingly unusual language with a clear interlinking text

Contents

What is aphasia? – 'Is frightened. Is frightened.': the early experience of stroke and aphasia – 'The thing is – what job?: work, leisure and aphasia – 'Can I get a word in edgeways?: family, friends and aphasia – 'Lost in the undertow': health, social care and voluntary services for people with aphasia – 'Everything seems a secret': information and aphasia – 'Doing the inside work': the meaning of aphasia – 'They cannot see it so how will they know?': aphasia and disability – 'I'm fed up of saying I'm sorry': learning to live with aphasia – Appendix: about the project – Further reading.

160pp   0 335 19936 4 (Paperback)   0 335 19937 2 (Hardback)

FEMALE FORMS
EXPERIENCING AND UNDERSTANDING DISABILITY

Carol Thomas

- What is the relevance of feminist ideas for understanding women's experiences of disability?
- How can the social model of disability be developed theoretically?
- What are the key differences between Disability Studies and medical sociology?

In answer to these questions, this book explores and develops ideas about disability, engaging with important debates in disability studies about what disability is and how to theorize it. It also examines the interface between disability studies, women's studies and medical sociology, and offers an accessible review of contemporary debates and theoretical approaches. The title *Female Forms* reflects two things about the book: first, its use of disabled women's experiences, as told by themselves, to bring a number of themes to life, and second, the author's belief in the importance of feminist ideas and debates for disability studies. The social model of disability is the book's bedrock, but the author both challenges and contributes to social modelist thought. She advances a materialist feminist perspective on disability, producing a book which is of multi-disciplinary relevance.

Female Forms will be useful to the growing number of students on Disability Studies courses, as well as those interested in women's studies, medical sociology and social policy. It will also appeal to those studying or working in the health and social care professions such as nursing, social work, occupational therapy and physiotherapy.

Contents
Introduction – Part I: Defining disability – Defining disability: the social model – Defining disability: a definitional riddle – Disability and the social self – Part II: Female forms – Disability and feminist perspectives: the personal and the political – Disability and gender – Wherein lies the difference? – Part III: Understanding disability – Theorizing disability and impairment – Disability studies and medical sociology – References – Index.

192pp   0 335 19693 4 (Paperback)   0 335 19694 2 (Hardback)